Opera Guide

Carmen
Bizet

Ann Howard as Carmen in the 1970 ENO production (photo: Donald Southern)

Preface

This series, published under the auspices of English National Opera and The Royal Opera, aims to prepare audiences to enjoy and evaluate opera performances. English National Opera is most grateful to Mobil for its generous sponsorship which has made this Guide possible. Each book contains the complete text, set out in the original language together with a current performing translation. The accompanying essays have been commissioned as general introductions to aspects of interest in each work. As many illustrations and musical examples as possible have been included because the sound and spectacle of opera are clearly central to any sympathetic appreciation of it. We hope that, as companions to the opera should be, they are well-informed, witty and attractive.

Nicholas John
Series Editor

Carmen

Georges Bizet

Opera Guide Series Editor: Nicholas John

Published in association with English National Opera and The Royal Opera

This Guide is sponsored by **M⊙bil**

John Calder · London
Riverrun Press · New York

First published in Great Britain, 1982, by
John Calder (Publishers) Ltd, 18 Brewer Street,
London W1R 4AS

and

First published in U.S.A., 1982, by
Riverrun Press Inc.,
175 Fifth Avenue
New York, NY 10010

BRITISH LIBRARY CATALOGUING IN PUBLICATION DATA
Bizet, Georges
    Carmen. — (Opera guide; 13)
    1. Bizet, Georges. Carmen 2. Operas — Librettos
    I. Title II. John, Nicholas III. Meilhac, Henri IV. Halévy, Ludovic V. Series
    782.1'092'4   ML410.B62
ISBN 0 7145 3937 6
Library of Congress Register

John Calder (Publishers) Ltd, English National Opera and
The Royal Opera House, Covent Garden Ltd receive financial
assistance from the Arts Council of Great Britain. English
National Opera also receives financial assistance from the
Greater London Council.

Typeset in Plantin by Margaret Spooner Typesetting, Dorchester, Dorset.

Printed and bound in Great Britain by Whitstable Litho Ltd., Whitstable, Kent.

Contents

List of Illustrations

Introduction

Nicholas John

'I shall be delighted to ... try to change the *genre* of *opéra-comique*. Down with *La Dame Blanche!*'
Bizet to Camille du Locle, director of the Opéra Comique, in 1869

Before the première of *Carmen* on March 3, 1875, Ludovic Halévy (one of the librettists) said 'the thing had little importance for Meilhac and me'. When Bizet died, at the age of thirty-six, just three months later, he knew that *Carmen* had failed to please both management and audience. And yet a century on we can see that it boasts one of the best texts ever written and has uncanny box-office appeal.

Célestine Galli-Marié, who had created the title role in Ambroise Thomas's 'Mignon' in 1866, created the title role of 'Carmen' in Paris in 1875, and sang it in 1886 for the first London performances in French.

Minnie Hauk, the first Carmen in London and New York. She refused to sing the role unless she was allowed to choose the rest of the cast including Campanini as Don José and Del Puente as Escamillo.

Bizet's *Carmen* disappointed expectations in various ways. One of the directors of the Opéra Comique resigned because, instead of the conventional happy ending, it finished with a murder. His colleagues were worried that the scabrous story would — as it did — offend their regular audiences. Their theatre had, in fact, gained a reputation as a place where the most proper of engaged couples could meet. Parents were happy to rely on the innocuous entertainment which *opéra-comique* had become.

The two librettists tried to soften the aspects of Bizet's chosen subject which might cause offence. Their collaboration, which lasted over twenty years, was notorious for their texts of Offenbach's satirical operettas, which were certainly *not* performed at the Opéra Comique. While *Carmen* was in rehearsal between October and December 1874, they had no less than four other works staged in Paris. Meilhac was a playwright, with little interest in music, who supplied the dialogue and the comic relief. Halévy, the nephew of Bizet's teacher and father-in-law, the opera composer Fromental Halévy, wrote the verses. Their published text of *Carmen* differs considerably from what Bizet set to music. They continually proposed refrains and rhyming couplets which would have been ideal for conventional *opéra-comique*, or indeed for Offenbach's routines, and Bizet 'ferociously' altered and rejected them. They suggested Zulma Bouffar, the star of many operettas — especially *La Vie Parisienne* — for the title role; and in rejecting her, Bizet and the Opéra Comique management at least agreed on one point.

Bizet certainly delighted in comedy. He welcomed a chance to introduce the choruses of urchins and gipsies, as much as the many other moments of parody and laughter into his score. His intentions in *Carmen* were, however, more serious than those of his management or librettists. Aware of the constraints of French musical conventions, his deeply-questioning genius looked beyond them for inspiration in other arts and other fields of thought. Six months after his marriage in 1869, he described his wife in words which seem to reflect himself:

> an adorable creature whose intelligence is open to all kinds of progress and reform, who believes neither in the God of the Jews nor in the God of the Christians, but in honour, duty, in a word morality.

This is the spirit which inspired *Carmen* and brought new life to *opéra-comique*.

Georges Bizet (Royal College of Music)

Opéra-Comique

Martin Cooper

We know exactly the date at which Italian opera was introduced into France and can follow the course of its naturalisation in the works of the gallicised Italian, Lully. The origins of the *opéra-comique*, on the other hand, are both more various and more difficult to trace, as we should expect in the case of a spontaneous indigenous art-form. They are to be found initially in the sideshows of the big Parisian fairs of the middle ages, the Foire Saint Germain and the Foire Saint Laurent — popular entertainments consisting of slapstick and patter, miming and dumb-show, intelligible to the slowest wit and often crudely indecent. Apart from rough dancing, the first musical element in these sideshows was to be found in the use of popular tunes whose words were so familiar that merely to hum the tune was enough to provide a wordless comment on a situation. Gags would be topical; and in fact the Italian opera introduced to the Court in the 1640s provided an excellent subject for parody, the taking-off of Lully's high-falutin' mythological *tragédies lyriques*, which soon became an accepted practice. This, and the imitation of the improvised dramas performed by travelling Italian troupes of the *commedia dell'arte* gave *opéra-comique* a clear, if still primitive, character of its own by the end of the seventeenth century.

No serious French musician interested himself in what remained part adaptation, part parody, with much improvisation and more speech than singing. Although Favart had already given the texts of these small pieces a literary character, it was not until an Italian company gave a season of *opera buffa* in 1752 that the possibility of creating a French equivalent in the *opéra-comique* seems to have occurred to French musicians. Even then the first properly 'composed' works were by an Italian, Duni, who wrote half a dozen successful *opéras-comiques* between 1955 and 1770.

Two quite distinct social groups championed the new form. The supporters of French as against Italian music were anxious to create a French equivalent of *opera buffa*, dealing with characters and situations drawn from everyday life instead of the gods, heroes and royal personages of the opera. At the same time what we should today call the left-wing intellectuals — thinkers and writers concerned with undermining the existing régime and preparing the ground for social and political revolution — were attracted by the naturalness and simplicity of form, its popular character and its use for thinly disguised social propaganda. Thus by the 1760s we find the peasant characters in the *opéras-comiques* of Philidor — cobbler, blacksmith, woodcutter — speaking their own countrified French and loudly voicing their resentment of the pretensions of squire, schoolmaster and local Justice. Jean-Jacques Rousseau's small piece, *Le Devin du Village* (*The Village Sorcerer*) — parodied by Mozart in *Bastien et Bastienne*, had its mild note of subversiveness, although Madame de Pompadour herself took part in one performance.

Opéra-comique, however, remained an essentially topical form, reflecting the changing fashions and preoccupations of each decade, so that social criticism soon gave way first to sentimental pastoral themes and, in the last years before the Revolution, to sentimental 'tear-jerkers' — *pièces à mouchoirs* or *comédies larmoyantes*, as they were called. If the sentimental pastorals

9

Edmond Clément as Don José (Stuart-Liff Collection)

found a parallel in Boucher's painting, such works as Monsigny's *'Le déserteur'* and Grétry's *'Lucile'* belong to the same world as Greuze's *'Cruche cassée'* and *'Oiseau mort'*.

Grétry was the most accomplished musician to dedicate himself entirely to the *opéra-comique*, and he explored its possibilities in many directions — among them fairy opera (*Zémire et Azor*), medievalism (*Aucassin et Nicolette*) and historical romance (*Richard Cœur de Lion*). These and other works of the '60s and '70s were given all over Europe, wherever Courts followed French fashions. Thus it came about that at Bonn, for instance, the young Beethoven grew up familiar with works by Monsigny and Grétry, while Gluck adapted or imitated fashionable Parisian pieces for the Viennese Court; and in Russia Catherine the Great characteristically employed these French imports for her own devious political purposes.

Although the Revolution was reflected in the *opéra-comique*, and the first Théâtre de l'Opéra Comique National was constituted in 1793, such topical works as Kreutzer's *August the Tenth, or the Fall of the Last Tyrant* and *The Reduction of Toulon* were essentially short-lived. One of the most popular works of the Revolutionary years was Devienne's *Les Visitandines* which, though marked by some mild and obvious 'blasphemies', is in effect no more

10

Zélie de Lussan as Carmen, a role she sang in New York and London

than the story of a young blood and his comic valet disguising themselves in order to remove the heroine from a convent. Sentiment was of course still fashionable, though it often took more heroic forms in 'rescue' operas, as in Gaveaux's setting of Bouilly's *Léonore, ou l'Amour conjugal*, which Beethoven was to transform into *Fidelio*.

The most important composer in France between 1790 and 1810 was the Italian Cherubini, whose *opéras-comiques* (especially *Les Deux Journées*) marked a new musical standard, matched by those of his contemporary Méhul but not by the more popular works of Boieldieu, Dalayrac (a pupil of Grétry's) or the Maltese Isouard, whose *Cendrillon* was a European success. It is interesting to find Carl Maria von Weber at this time accepting the *opéra-comique* — which he describes as 'conversation-opera' — and discussing it in the same breath as Italian *opera seria* and that ideal German opera which he spent his life in shaping and developing.

The relationship between opera and *opéra-comique* changed after the Revolution. The operas written by Gluck during the 1770s were the highest musical achievement of the *ancien régime* in France and they marked the end of a musical as well as a social era. The spirit of the Revolution, which found expression in the *opéra-comique*, was essentially alien to the formal, aristo-

11

cratic splendours associated with opera, but something to take the place of those splendours was soon required by the Napoleonic Empire. It was provided not by Cherubini, but by another Italian, Spontini, whose *Fernand Cortez* was a deliberate piece of propaganda, martial and magnificent, designed to influence the public in favour of Napoleon's Spanish campaign. When similar historical themes were treated, with a maximum of scenic display, by Auber in *La Muette de Portici* and by Rossini in *Guillaume Tell*, 'French grand opera' was launched; and it only needed the works written by Meyerbeer during the 1830s to achieve a European significance. None of this was without influence on the *opéra-comique*. The new fashion for historical subjects initiated by the novels of Walter Scott, and very much in tune with the mood of the Bourbon Restoration, had been anticipated by Grétry's *Richard Cœur de Lion* (1784) and reappeared in Boieldieu's *Jean de Paris* (1812). Boieldieu took the subject of his most successful work, *La Dame Blanche*, from Scott and Auber, who was to become the leading *opéra-comique* composer from 1840 to 1870, did the same with his *Leicester, ou le Château de Kenilworth*. *Opéra-comique* was in fact losing many of its original, specifically French, characteristics — the rural or domestic setting, the often sophisticated 'innocence' of the characters and the wit which had distinguished the best pre-revolutionary librettists, Favart and Sedaine. These 'conversation-pieces', with their often primitive music, were still produced in plenty but perhaps the last to be still remembered today, Adam's *Le Postillon de Longjumeau*, dates from 1836. The great successes of *opéra-comique* in the 1830s were melo-dramatically 'romantic' and set in exotic scenery — Hérold's *Zampa* and Auber's *Fra Diavolo*, *Le Domino noir* and *Les Diamants de la couronne*. Hérold's *Le Pré aux clercs* was a miniature *opéra-comique* companion-piece to Meyerbeer's *Les Huguenots*.

Sheet music front for a quadrille arranged from the score showing the original Opéra Comique production and Carmen about to throw her flower at Don José. (Raymond Mander and Joe Mitchenson Theatre Collection)

Frasquita warns Carmen to take care — a print of the first interpreters of the roles. (Raymond Mander and Joe Mitchenson Theatre Collection)

The feature that remained unchanged, and was often the only rigid distinction between opera and *opéra-comique*, was the spoken dialogue. This was deeply rooted in the common French conception of music as something essentially secondary, either an accompaniment to dancing and spectacle, or an interlude, as in the old *comédie mêlée d'ariettes*. French taste in the matter was firmly realistic and easily sniffed the ridiculous in sung recitative, as it had earlier in the antics — and indeed the very existence — of the *castrato* singers. By 1830, when Rossini boasted that Italian training and Italian vocal standards had revolutionised French singing, only the more simple-minded audiences were still satisfied by the simple ditties and primitive orchestration associated with the old *opéra-comique*, and Parisian *mélomanes* for the next two generations were to favour the Théâtre-Italien, which acquired the social cachet once enjoyed by the Opéra. It was the bourgeois who kept the *opéra-comique* alive during those years, and their favourite was Auber.

The twenty-five works produced by Auber between 1830 and his death in 1871 were written to a formula elaborated by the composer and his chief librettist, Scribe, the greatest theatrical craftsman of his day. They were marked by physical verve and easy predictability in rhythms and melodies, primitive harmonic schemes and that self-complacent wit, both verbal and in this case musical, that has always been characteristic of the Parisian bourgeois. Emotionally Auber's music is empty, and this is perhaps the chief reason for its failure to compete with the new operetta introduced by Offenbach and immediately successful during the 1850s, the first years of Napoleon the Third's Second Empire. Saint-Saens described operetta as a 'daughter of *opéra-comique*, but a daughter who has gone to the bad'. It would be truer, perhaps, to see it as a revival of what had once been a major ingredient of *opéra-comique*, namely satire, both political and social; and it was this that

Emma Calvé as Carmen in 1893 in New York. Heard at the Opéra Comique for the first time in 1892, her performance became a fad in America. Herman Klein noted that her interpretation combined the most fascinating characteristics of all her predecessors. 'It had the calm, easy assurance, the calculated, dominating power of Galli-Mariè's; it had the strong sensual suggestion and defiant resolution of Minnie Hauk's; it had the pantherlike quality, the grace, the fatalism, the dangerous, impudent coquetry of Pauline Lucca's; it had the sparkle, the vim, the Spanish insouciance and piquancy of Zélie de Lussan's.' (Raymond Mander and Joe Mitchenson Theatre Collection)

gave Offenbach's works the piquancy, the relevance and the novelty which the *opéra-comique* had lost. As early as 1837 Théophile Gautier has described *opéra-comique* as 'that wretched bastard form composed of two incompatible elements, in which actors excuse their bad acting by saying that they are singers and sing out of tune on the plea that they are actors'. Nearly twenty years later Adolphe Adam could still boast that, in writing for the theatre 'my only ambition is to write music which is transparent, easy to understand and amusing to the public', which is the fundamental ambition of all writers of entertainment-music in any age. Offenbach's advantage lay in the fact that he shocked his audiences as well as amusing them.

Even so, with much of its public lost to the new operetta and its distinction from opera all but vanished, *opéra-comique* continued its independent existence. The opening of the new Théâtre Lyrique in 1851 gave it something like a new lease of life, for this was a theatre in which new works were accepted on their merits rather than according to the formal genres to which they belonged. It was here that Gounod's *Faust* was given in its original form with spoken dialogue, as well as the unpretentious *Le Médecin malgré lui* and *Philémon et Baucis* in which much of the old *opéra-comique* spirit survived. In the same theatre Bizet's first two operas were produced, *Les Pêcheurs de perles* and *La Jolie Fille de Perth*, and it was more by chance than by design that both his *Djamileh* and *Carmen* were given not at the Théâtre Lyrique but at the Opéra Comique itself. If *Djamileh* belonged to an *opéra-comique* tradition by its slightness and its conversational tone in an exotic setting, *Carmen's* links with the form are no more than vestigial.

Bizet was by no means a 'reformer' by temperament, and he was more anxious to discover an outlet for his talents which would also provide him with a formula for popular success than with altering the course of musical history. Auber's death in 1871 marked the end of an era in the history of the *opéra-comique* and the genre itself was felt by many musicians to be beyond rescuing. It was certainly something totally different from Auber that Bizet had in mind when he wrote in 1869 of 'trying to change the genre of *opéra-comique*' although his 'down with *La Dame Blanche!*' was aimed rather at Boieldieu. Bizet's motives were no doubt mixed. He made no secret of his desire for popular success, but he wanted to combine this with the full exercise of his talents. The death of the old *opéra-comique* seemed to leave a gap in the French musical scene which he was anxious to fill.

The subject matter of Mérimée's story, though an obvious invitation to full operatic treatment, did not by the standards of the day exclude the lighter form. The two most recent successes in *opéra-comique*, Gounod's *Faust* and Thomas's *Mignon*, were after all drawn from Goethe. In fact Bizet's librettists were famous for their collaboration in Offenbach's greatest triumphs including *La Belle Hélène*, *La Vie Parisienne*, *La Grande-Duchesse de Gerolstein* and *La Périchole*; and *Carmen*, coming from such a source, might have been expected to err if anything in the direction of operetta rather than opera. It proved, however, that it was his librettists rather than Bizet himself who were nervous of adhering too closely to Mérimée's story, foreseeing the scandal of staging such a tale at the Opéra Comique, traditionally the scene of family outings. The essential innovation in *Carmen* lies in Bizet's attitude towards the character of Carmen herself. In the theatre, if not in literature, a heroic — or anti-heroic — stand outside the law and morality had hitherto been a male privilege: Mozart's *Don Giovanni* is a case in point. Violetta's role in *La traviata*, for instance, was acceptably balanced by Germont Père's moralising and, of course, her death. In the *opéra-comique*, even more perhaps than elsewhere in the theatre, women were expected to be gentle, biddable,

15

always sinned against but never sinning — with the single exception of the 'sweetest sin of the seven' for which they were always made to pay heavily, as did Marguérite in Gounod's *Faust*.

When the librettists invented the character of Micaela to illustrate José's youthful innocence and to contrast with Carmen, and further developed Escamillo as a foil to José, they were in fact continuing a tradition of the *opéra-comique*. Micaela is not only the conventional 'sweet girl', but her arrival with a letter from the hero's mother is an echo of Meyerbeer's *Robert le Diable* in which Alice, whose music has the simple, quasi-popular character of the old *opéra-comique*, appears on the same errand. Both Micaela and Escamillo are given music that is conventional — in fact very reminiscent of Gounod — compared with the rest of the opera; but it is for their conventional characters that they are in fact needed dramatically. Bizet is careful to suggest this in the case of Escamillo, when he marks the refrain (*'Toreador, en garde!'*) of Escamillo's *couplets* in Act Two with the words *avec fatuité* — that is to say, 'with almost ludicrous self-complacency'. If there is a long way between Mérimée's principals — Carmen a thief and a liar, as well as a drab, and José a triple murderer and the characters in the opera, this was inevitable in 1875. (Producers might still, however, bear in mind that Mérimée describes José as looking like Milton's Satan.) The gap between the original tale and the opera is still further widened by abandoning the spoken dialogue, which not only explained a number of details of the plot but in many instances preserved Mérimée's own words. The sung recitatives with which we are familiar were provided by the composer's old friend, Ernest Guiraud, for the first performance of the work in Vienna, in October 1875, some three months after Bizet's death. They contain nothing musically or dramatically objectionable and provide the best solution to a problem which is in fact insoluble. The art of spoken dialogue does not form part of the opera-singer's training as such in any country but France; and it is even arguable that to translate French dialogue into another language (and then have it spoken amateurishly) is in every sense worse than singing it, whether in French or not.

Sung dialogue does not convert *Carmen* into a 'French grand opera'. We know from the case of Gounod's *Faust* that it takes more to do that, for when *Faust* was transferred from the Théâtre Lyrique to the Opéra it was not only the sung recitatives (which had been added for a Strasbourg production the year after the work appeared) but the addition of a ballet that transformed the original and added that element of pure inorganic spectacle characteristic of 'grand' opera. Historically, however, the introduction of Guiraud's recitatives proved misleading to a later generation, the Italian followers of *verismo*, who claimed *Carmen* as the source of their realistic operatic ideals. Now, by the same kind of posthumous contagion which has led to Rachmaninov and Ravel somehow sounding like Hollywood composers, productions of *Carmen* too often present it as a kind of *Cavalleria rusticana* or, as in the film version conducted by Karajan, a smart, velvety *turistico* affair in the Italian manner. Certainly French spoken dialogue is the greatest possible safeguard against this kind of deformation; but where that is impracticable, as it is in all but francophone countries, both conductor and producer can do much to ensure the French character of the work by avoiding all exaggeration in the style of scenery, acting and, most importantly of all, singing. Bizet must never be made to sound — or 'look' — like Puccini. Whether *Carmen* is in any sense an *opéra-comique* has long been a purely academic point, but that Bizet lies plumb in the middle of the French conception of sonority is an important practical fact.

Enrico Caruso as Don José (Teatro alla Scala)

Ann Howard as Carmen in the 1970 ENO production (photo: Donald Southern)

A Musical Commentary

Lesley A. Wright

'People make me out to be obscure, complicated, tedious, more fettered by technical skill than lit by inspiration. Well, this time I have written a work that is all clarity and vivacity, full of colour and melody. It will be entertaining . . .' Bizet expected immediate success for the vibrant work he began to compose in 1873. He had suggested the subject, Mérimée's *Carmen*, to his librettists, Henri Meilhac and Ludovic Halévy, and worked closely with them to create (and even contribute directly to) the libretto so that he might control the crucial balance of music and drama. The synthesis of the two arts, however, did not materialize immediately. Bizet normally revised extensively during rehearsal, but for *Carmen* this period was particularly extended, difficult and productive of brilliant second thoughts. The finales of Acts One, Three and Four were each reworked several times. Several solo numbers were revised or rewritten. The role of the chorus was reduced and its entrances and exits adjusted. And there were many more changes of detail. He altered or thinned scoring and showed a keen interest in specifying precise tempo markings to heighten dramatic impact (as in the closing scene where alternating tempi further contrast the on-stage tragedy and off-stage rejoicing). The sum of such changes produced a final reading of strikingly effective drama and concise, intensely expressive, music.

Bizet himself reduced the orchestral score (incorporating rehearsal changes and adding further refinements) and read proofs for the Choudens piano-vocal score issued shortly after the March 3, 1875 première. Here he decided on the final form of the opera he wished to present to the public. Yet, except for the initial run of performances at the Opéra Comique, *Carmen* has seldom been presented as we know Bizet authorised it: an *opéra-comique* with a *Prélude* and twenty-seven pieces, most separated by scenes in spoken dialogue.

Only a few months after Bizet's death sources began to omit the *Scène et Pantomime* (Act One) and cut half the José-Escamillo duet (Act Three), changes possibly attributable to the composer. Bizet had also signed a contract with the Vienna Opera to compose recitatives for their performances of October 1875; but since his death intervened, his friend Ernest Guiraud wrote them in a compatible style. Despite competent workmanship, the compression of dialogue removed some necessary explanations and considerably reduced subtlety in characterisation, especially for minor characters. Furthermore, Bizet had constructed many pieces to build out of and fade into the spoken dialogue around them; although Guiraud carefully avoided tampering with these areas, Bizet might well have done more here to integrate added recitatives with the existing score. Guiraud also modified the opening chorus of the last act to accommodate a ballet concocted from *La Jolie Fille de Perth* (1866-1867) and the incidental music to *L'Arlésienne* (1872). All these changes appear in the Bizet-Guiraud hybrid, published in full and piano-vocal score by Choudens about 1877; and, in this form, *Carmen* conquered the opera stages of the world.

In 1964, a critical edition of *Carmen* opened up many new performance options, for Fritz Oeser had discovered the original orchestral parts and conductor's score, stored in a dusty cupboard at the Opéra Comique. They had somehow survived the disastrous fire of 1887 and were used through the 1890s until they were replaced by engraved parts, set aside and forgotten. With these materials Oeser completed missing orchestration for the *Pantomime* and Act Three duet and brought to light many earlier versions, some completely unknown. In preparing this score, however, he virtually ignored the testimony of Bizet's 1875 piano-vocal score. Instead, he included in his main volume itself readings from rejected earlier layers and discarded stage directions from the materials he located; more importantly, he relegated Bizet's final readings to convoluted textual notes (or appendices) from which they may be retrieved only with difficulty.While some twenty larger passages of this type are easily identified, Oeser's consistent preference for placing earlier readings in the main score has also altered hundreds of details, some quite damaging to the work's vitality. Certain passages cut during rehearsal may be welcomed back for their intrinsic beauty, not just their novelty. There is a constant danger, nonetheless, that reinstating too many of the earlier versions or details (which may be done quite unintentionally due to Oeser's editorial policy) may cause the action to drag, particularly in the First Act, and crucial scenes to lose their dramatic impact.

Each production of *Carmen* will represent a different set of conclusions about the optimum combination of so many choices; but since Bizet supervised the preparation of only one score and never indicated dissatisfaction with it, analysis of his 1875 version forms the basis of this commentary.

*

Carmen opens with a brilliantly scored *Prélude* in A-major that immediately reveals Bizet's great skill in orchestration. As Richard Strauss said, 'If you want to learn how to orchestrate . . . study the score of *Carmen*. What wonderful economy, and how every note and rest is in its proper place.' Strings form the basis of Bizet's orchestra while brass and the distinctive timbres of woodwind are used largely for striking effects. (Thus the low range of the flute is reserved for Carmen's seductive moods, and the mournful English horn appears only three times in the entire score.) The orchestral texture has consummate grace and clarity and ranges to extremes (from the overstated Toreador Song to the transparent delicacy of the Act Three *entr'acte*) for purposes of characterisation or drama. The opening section of the *Prélude*, with crashing percussion and full scoring, is deliberately blatant and popular in order to anticipate the atmosphere of the last Act. It quotes from the march [1,2] which accompanies the procession of Escamillo, the Toreador, to the bullfight. A contrasting section switches abruptly to F-major and Escamillo's refrain [17], where, at first, strings play the melody in octaves and the brass alone provides the accompaniment (unusual orchestration for Bizet's period). A brief return to the opening idea closes the musical form, and a pause suggests that the piece has finished; but then, without transition, the most developed presentation of the 'fate motif' [3a] sounds *fortissimo*, darkly scored and immediately memorable through its emphasis on the exotic augmented second. The motif is identified with Carmen's fatal influence on Don José; it is always restricted to the orchestra and is used most tellingly once only in each act, every time rescored or varied. Though the entrance and interaction of the principal characters is delayed, their fate has already been suggested, and we return suddenly to everyday Seville.

At a deliberately leisurely pace, the first few pieces of Act One establish the routines of life in that city; the later numbers show how Carmen, a gipsy exempt from society's rules, disrupts its routines and powerfully affects those around her. A deftly orchestrated, but otherwise conventional, male chorus

Act One in the 1903 Opéra Comique production designed by Jusseaume (Royal Opera House Archives)

framing a section largely for soloists begins the act. Like most act-opening numbers, it functions mainly to create atmosphere and conveys minimal information. Bored soldiers watch passers-by [4] until Micaela's entry (to light triplets) provides them with an opportunity to flirt. We learn only that she is looking for Don José and that he will arrive with the changing of the guard [5]. Her exit spurs a return to their previous pastime and music.

In the 1875 score, the soldiers continue this activity through the rarely performed *Scéne et Pantomime*, a charming solo piece in three strophes. There the officer in charge, Morales, comments ironically upon an apparently proper young wife escorted by her elderly husband. In the course of their stroll she contrives (groups of grace notes illustrate her slyness) to receive a billet-doux from her lover. Although it was standard practice in *opéra-comique* to follow an *Introduction* by a solo number, the *Pantomime* serves a dramatic function as well in its depiction of a love triangle (with an old lover replaced by a new one) that foreshadows the involvement of Carmen, José and Escamillo.

Without intervening dialogue, a cornet announces the arrival of the *'garde-montante'* (and Don José). The jaunty, regularly-phrased tune first appears, distinctively scored, as a high piccolo duet [6] over cornet and plucked strings, and Bizet continues to vary the delicate orchestration masterfully throughout the children's two-part march. Much of the second section and parts of the orchestral close were cut in rehearsals (for the sole dramatic purpose was

Design by Edward Burra for the opening act of the 1947 production of 'Carmen' at Covent Garden. (Royal Opera House Archives)

served when José arrived on-stage). Also removed was a lovely canon (on [6]) for solo violin and cello that once connected the two strophes under the Morales-José conversation.

In a more conventional arrangement José might have arrived singing *couplets* on the joys or rigours of a soldier's life, with the male chorus participating in the refrain; but he sings very little in Act One, and not at all until after Carmen has disturbed his composure. The humorous chorus for children alone, on the other hand, is extremely unusual in French opera and

The 1968/69 production of 'Carmen' at Covent Garden with George Macpherson as Zuniga and Heather Harper as Micaela. (photo: Houston Rogers)

Laurence Dale as Don José and Véronique Dietschy as Micaela in Peter Brook's production in the Bouffes du Nord, Paris, 1981 (photo: Nicolas Treatt)

particularly memorable because Bizet, like Debussy, had a special affinity for portraits of children in a music at once accessible and deceptively simple. Shortly after the children have marched off, the tobacco factory bell rings. In another daily ritual the admirers of the female workers enter, express their anticipation and then approval to *arpeggios* in muted strings and a rising woodwind melody that suggests drifting cigarette smoke. A relaxed tempo and smooth line [7] portray the seductive languor of the cigarette-smoking women. Because some acting was involved, the chorus caused great problems in rehearsal; perhaps related to this, Bizet cut an attractive central section in which the tenors begged for attention. Now, however, the men sing fervently only as they ask after the missing Carmencita. The higher dynamic level, shorter phrases and faster tempo indicate both their excitement and Carmen's much stronger effect on men than any of the women introduced previously (a gradation from the naive Micaela, to the duplicitous *bourgeoise*, to the cigarette-smoking factory workers). Strings present her theme [3b] with an augmented second that gives a gipsy flavour as she enters and adroitly manages her admirers. Like its variant [3a], her theme is sparingly used in later scenes to maximise its dramatic effectiveness. Anecdotes maintain that

Bizet rewrote Carmen's entrance piece thirteen times before he could please his first Carmen, Galli-Marié. While the number may be exaggerated, a fragment of one earlier version's refrain, a banal A-minor tune in 6/8, suggests that he did not always exploit exotic colour so memorably. The music here must be as hypnotic as the woman herself or the reactions she produces in men generally and in José specifically will not be believable. To this end, Bizet penned the vivid metaphors with which Carmen describes herself. Although Spanish and Portuguese settings had called forth Boleros and Seguidillas before, the *Habañera* rhythm was new to *opéra-comique*. Bizet did not write a typically French melody above the rhythm but borrowed one by a Spanish-American composer, Yradier. The *Habañera* breaks no new ground in its form. Similar to Escamillo's *couplets* in Act Two, it has two strophes ([8], in D-minor), each followed by a refrain ([9], in D-major). The chorus adds variety to the regular four-bar phrasing. By adding a triplet, prolonging the sinuous chromatic descent in the strophe and varying the repetitive refrain, Bizet transformed Yradier's melody; and the uninterrupted, sensuous Cuban dance rhythm, based on a low-D pedal note and a relatively limited harmonic vocabulary, sustains its mesmerizing tension.

When Carmen has finished, the men take up their pleading again; but Carmen has noticed José, who pays no attention to her. The significance of their first confrontation is underlined by [3a]. Carmen approaches José, speaks to him provocatively over two sustained notes in the violas, and on a dissonant chord throws a flower at him and runs off, followed by the other factory workers who laughingly sing [9]. The factory bell sounds again, but this time the orchestra comments in a soaring melody on José's emotions as he picks up the flower. Her theme [3b] flickers downward in the orchestra, both to make it clear that her charms have already bewitched José, despite his suspicions of this *'sorcière'*, and to reinforce the relationship of the two themes

[3a, 3b], which are never again used in the same scene. Bizet's first thoughts for this incident were more melodramatic, with lingering looks and no spoken text, but during rehearsals Bizet cut the extended use of [3a], presumably at the time he wrote the *Prélude* and decided to place the music there, rescored.

Before José has time to regain his composure, Micaela [10] enters, reintroduced as a foil to Carmen and as a representative of Don José's conservative world (a religious mother, a Basque village, and a pure girl). José sings for the first time, in the same smooth conventional melodies as Micaela [12]. Although they sing what sounds superficially like a standard love duet, José, eager for news of his mother, and Micaela, scarcely more than a messenger from this influential figure, they say very little directly to one another. The depth of the mother-son relationship is portrayed in quasi-religious music, accompanied by the usual harp *arpeggios* [11]. When José thinks of his mother as a guardian angel against the '*démon*', Carmen's theme sounds in the orchestra. Micaela leaves, embarrassed by a letter in which José's mother advises him to marry her; he, a dutiful son, immediately swears to do so and is about to throw away Carmen's flower.

But a squabble breaks out in the tobacco factory, and the dramatic pace speeds again. Like angry bees the women stream onto the stage. The two groups exchange short phrases, with vocal entries quite difficult to co-ordinate with the required staging, even for today's performers. (In 1875, the Opéra Comique singers, used to standing still and facing the conductor like an oratorio chorus, nearly foundered on this piece). They describe a quarrel between Manuelita and Carmencita; and Zuniga, the lieutenant, sends José into the factory to investigate. He reappears with the defiantly guilty Carmen, to the passionate tune that sounded earlier, now intensified by an expressive countermelody in violas and high cellos. José, encountering Carmen again so soon, is profoundly disturbed by her personal magnetism. Bizet originally

Ileana Cotrubas as Micaela and Jon Vickers as Don José at Covent Garden (photo: Donald Southern)

introduced their entrance in the middle of the reprise of the chorus. While musically interesting, this provided no dramatic rationale for the return of José's melody to close the piece, and Bizet, aware of the great length of the First Act, may have cut the section during rehearsals for this reason. When Zuniga (always speaking) questions Carmen about the fracas, she refuses to answer, and impertinently sings a tune [13] instead. A flute, in its distinctive low range, then a solo violin, and finally the cellos, echo her and portray the insolence of her manner. She seems to epitomise the threat of the rebel to authority and of a strong woman to the domination of men. As a last resort Zuniga orders José to take her to prison, and her motif [3b] sounds in the low flute and clarinet as she senses that her only opportunity to escape lies with this young *brigadier*. Unable to manipulate José by appealing to his sympathy or pretending to be Basque, Carmen resorts to song and dance, and conquers him by first hinting and then promising to become his lover.

It is in the final scene of each act that the José-Carmen relationship is developed before us, and the *Séguedille* [14] first establishes the pattern. Formal musical conventions (as well as the conventional *opéra-comique* plots) are strained or abandoned. The *Séguedille* opens as a delicately accompanied and gracefully harmonized solo piece. As in the *Habañera*, a dance rhythm and plucked strings suggest a guitar. A prominent part for the flute, particularly in its sensuous lower range, emphasizes Carmen's alluring sexuality; at one point it even dances along with her in a brief canon. The tune, however, is only the introduction to the crucial seduction scene which sets the tragedy in motion. Still based largely on the *Séguedille* melody and rhythm, it explores the dramatic resources of recitative, duet and particularly fluid harmony to make Carmen's persuasiveness irresistible and José's wavering and ultimate capitulation quite realistic. Once she is sure of him, she sings her song of seduction once more, this time triumphantly and in full voice. Immediately, muted strings introduce a wonderful four-voice fugue in F-minor (with a subject drawn from the quarrel chorus), whose contrapuntal interweavings both accompany and symbolise Carmen's plottings with José. The plans complete, the fugue breaks off and Carmen mocks Zuniga with her *Habañera* refrain [9], accompanied by sustained chords in D-flat that generate suspense. The text is ironically appropriate, for 'l'amour' is the agent of her release, and José, by rights should 'prends garde'. The tune, in delicate chromatic harmonisation, trips along in flutes and clarinet until Carmen finally pushes José and escapes. To general laughter, the full orchestra plays with the opening bars of the fugue subject, now in A-major, in a rollicking close.

Before Act Two we hear Don José's jaunty military tune [21] which, with subtle harmony and delightful counterpoint of clarinet and bassoon, contrasts José's world with Carmen's in the following *Chanson Bohème*. The curtain rises on a tavern of ill repute in the late evening. Flutes in thirds quietly introduce whirling figures of the gipsy dance. A harp and plucked strings imitate guitar accompaniment, and passing dissonances and distinctive harmonisation add a touch of the Spanish idiom without dependence on any borrowed source. The entire piece accelerates in a great *crescendo* and closes with frenetic dances. This *tour de force* of orchestration, one of the most impressive in all opera, is built around the three strophes Carmen sings [15], joined by Frasquita and Mercedes.

In conversation, Carmen learns from her new admirer Zuniga that José has just been released from a month in prison. A male chorus praising Escamillo, the toreador, is heard, first unaccompanied and backstage; then, invited by Zuniga, the toreador and his followers enter Pastia's tavern. The worshipping

26

Act Two in John Copley's production, designed by Stefanos Lazaridis, for ENO in 1970. (photo: Houston Rogers)

entourage, the flamboyant entry, and the deliberately bombastic music portray the vanity and self-confidence of this fourth protagonist. The conventional piece, brilliantly scored, consists of two strophes ([16], in F-minor), which describe a bullfight. The tortuous descent to a low B-flat, which opens this section, was designed to show off the exceptional range and strong low voice of the first Escamillo, Bouhy. The pompous refrain of his entrance aria ([17], in F-major, marked *'piano avec fatuité'*), which refers to the love of a woman awaiting the toreador after each combat, becomes Escamillo's signature tune. Even without encouragement (in contrast to José), Escamillo tells Carmen that her charms have attracted him (both in the dialogue and in the brief exchange on *'l'amour'* just before the close of the number). She does not encourage his attentions, although she makes it clear that his luck might improve later on. He and his followers leave to his refrain ([17] in E-major), just as Carmen and the factory workers left to her refrain [9] in the First Act. (Escamillo's grand entrance and departure were substantially shortened during rehearsals.)

The stage cleared, Carmen, Frasquita and Mercedes welcome their fellow smugglers Le Dancaïre and Le Remendado and conduct business in a delightful quintet. To create this masterpiece in the *opera buffa* tradition of Mozart and Rossini, Bizet makes use of transparent orchestration, rapid declamation, close harmonies and shifting groupings of the voices. The ideas of the opening section [18, 19] are reworked to accompany much of the middle

27

Act Two in John Copley's production for ENO designed by Stefanos Lazaridis with Katherine Pring in the title role. (photo: Donald Southern)

section. There Carmen astonishes her compatriots by announcing with genuine intensity (particularly striking in the comic context) that she is in love, and therefore cannot leave that evening. Le Dancaïre and Le Remendado [20] cajole her to *'faire marcher le devoir et l'amour'* – to reconcile love and duty, an ironic reference to the themes of classical French tragedy – but she, as always, is resolved to do as she pleases. A return to [19], praising women for their aptitude at intrigue, provides a brilliant finish.

Scarcely have Carmen's friends suggested that she might at least persuade her new lover to join their band than José arrives. By contrast with Escamillo, he enters alone, singing his simple (G-minor/G-major) military tune unaccompanied and largely backstage. Loss of rank and a month in jail have not cooled his desire for Carmen. Despite a touch of bravado, there is much touching, youthful vulnerability in his character. Bizet treats him in a different way from the other principals: his personality is not established immediately with a formal entrance aria. His music contrasts with the defined forms given to the music of Escamillo and Micaela and his character development is marked by increasingly unconventional musical patterns. For a reunion such as this an operatic couple would normally sing a standard love duet, praising the circumstances that brought them together and looking forward to a sublime future. The characters (with such conflicting expectations of each other) that were sharply drawn in Act One predispose this relationship, however, to fireworks. The duet starts calmly enough when

The Quintet with Teresa Cahill, Francis Egerton, Shirley Verrett, John Dobson, and Anne Pashley at Covent Garden (photo: Reg Wilson)

Carmen, with mock formality, announces that she will dance for José to calm his jealousy at the idea that she had entertained the other soldiers at the tavern. Midway through her voluptuous wordless singing, accompanied by castanets [22], two cornets backstage play the call to barracks. The remarkable counterpoint of these two musical elements symbolises José's predicament — a classic choice of *devoir* or *amour*. Carmen, unequivocally committed to *amour*, misunderstands when José first interrupts her and takes up her tune again. The call to barracks continues uninterrupted through their conversation and ends as Carmen realises that José actually intends to leave. A clarinet on its lowest note signals her amazement. She lashes out with wild recriminations, like a disappointed child, and absolutely refuses to listen to José's plaintive protestations — an appropriately realistic way to carry on an argument. (During rehearsal Bizet cut a section here in which Carmen mocked José by repeating his music in a different key.) The 'love duet' has already degenerated to a quarrel. José forces Carmen to listen to him; he is no longer so passive and tongue-tied as before. He bares his soul in five quatrains of poetry set to the smooth, continuous music of the Flower Song [23]. This piece does not reflect the musical language of the man who sang with Micaela nor the standard *couplet* form provided by the librettists.* José has already

---

* The librettists supplied six quatrains, in two stanzas, but Bizet cut the refrain 'Car tu n'avais eu qu'à paraître' from the end of the first. A typical example of his intention to avoid formal, conventional effects.

changed, and the orchestra offers further evidence of Carmen's profound effect on him: just before José's outburst, in a quiet, poignant presentation of the fate motif [3a] on the plangent English horn, and under the virtually whispered last phrase (*'Carmen, je t'aime'*), an arresting bar of foreign harmony in the woodwind. Despite pressure from the Opéra Comique management, Bizet did not provide for applause at this point (or later in the duet), preferring instead to emphasize Carmen's abrupt change of key to suggest the emotional distance between them in this continuous argument.

She now introduces more calculated tactics, similar to those she used in the *Séguedille*. As French horns evoke the countryside and strings add a galloping figure, she paints a seductive picture of a vagabond life together [24]. José protests weakly against her tune and surrenders — here flutes signal her victory and four quiet chords in the strings recall the foreign harmonies of the Flower Song cadence. But his surrender is only momentary. Unable to bear the loss of his soldier's honour, he bids adieu. The duet has apparently ended, without a repetition of the ensemble section [24] that normally closed duets at that time. The finale begins immediately as Zuniga knocks and enters, uninvited. Jealousy flaring, José not only refuses to leave but attacks his superior officer; he is prevented from doing him physical harm only by the arrival of the *bohémiens*. In a scene typical of the jolly brigands of the *opéra-comique* tradition, Carmen, Le Dancaïre and Le Remendado invite Zuniga to take a walk with them (presumably until the smugglers can leave in the opposite direction). Their pretended courtesy is emphasised by impertinent flute parts and a comic bassoon line. Ideas from the ensemble section of the duet return when Carmen, triumphant as at the end of the previous Act, invites José once more to join the smugglers. With the return of the ensemble music it becomes clear that the duet form has been greatly expanded to include the entire finale. The music, originally seductive, is transformed by context

George Wakewitch's design for Act Three in the 1953 Covent Garden production. (photo: Donald Southern)

Joseph Schwarz as Escamillo   *Licia Albanese as Micaela*

and tempo to a rousing anthem in praise of *'la liberté'*. Even José joins in at the close. He has chosen love over duty, but only when compelled to do so as a consequence of jealousy and uncontrollable temper, the character flaws that detonate the tragedy.

Act Three opens with a poetic evocation of a peaceful countryside. The smooth melody [25], typical of Bizet's extraordinary gift, is given new colours by the woodwind. While the piece becomes gradually more contrapuntal, it retains its transparency, and a secondary melody unfolds and develops in the strings. The contrapuntal texture fades away to a high *pianissimo* chord; and then, a note repeated twice, presumably a signal among the smugglers, raises the curtain on darkness and the C-minor chorus. A rhythmically nervous melody [26] accompanies their entrance, and a trudging, climbing bass represents their progress over a steep mountain pass. The dynamic level of the chorus is generally low, conspiratorial, except at the boldly chromatic harmonies of the warning, *'Prends garde de faire un faux pas'*. The soloists, who sing alone in the central section, are more sanguine and praise their *'métier'*, but the number as a whole is dark, like the emotions that surface in this Act.

In the dialogue José tries to make amends for an earlier argument; instead they argue again and Carmen predicts he will kill her. José, in keeping with his conservative Basque upbringing, has attempted to dominate and control his woman, while Carmen chafes under any restriction of her freedom. She turns to Frasquita and Mercedes, who amuse themselves by mock seriously reading their fortunes in the cards [27]. Each sees a happy future graced by love or riches — the climax is the delicious line *'Ah! je suis veuve et j'hérite!'* (literally: 'Ah! I am widowed and I inherit!'). When Carmen picks up the cards,

31

everything changes. Low-pitched brass octaves foreshadow the dark fate she will read — death for herself, then José. It is a fate that will inevitably result from the extreme incompatibility of their natures, rather than any supernatural force. Her theme [3b] appears as she reads death, twice. She is not afraid, but stoically accepts her fate, and sings a simple melody [28] to Bizet's own straightforward lyrics. Heavy brass is gradually added to the repeated chords as they seem to crush her in their slow even rhythm. When Frasquita and Mercedes return to their prattling refrain [27], Carmen's voice continues below theirs, reading death in the cards. Her theme [3b] reappears in low strings as the number closes. Carmen's prophecy, an intuitive analysis of her lover's character, has an impact so powerful that it hangs menacingly over the rest of the opera even though specific musical reference does not recur. At one stage, Bizet quoted from [28] in the finales of both Act Three and Act Four, but rejected the idea as too melodramatic.

A spirited ensemble piece [29] releases the tension. Carmen gaily agrees to join her friends in diverting the guards at the city walls so that the smugglers and their contraband may pass. Once the stage is empty Micaela, again used as a foil to Carmen, enters with her guide, searching for José. She sings the only solo piece in Act Three, a conventional Gounodesque aria framed by beautiful French horn writing. She prays [30] for protection; the rushing cello *arpeggios* illustrate her fear. Her strong vocal lines make her courage clear, especially as she imagines a confrontation with Carmen [31]. This moment of repose precedes one of the most dramatic sequences in the opera. Micaela hides when José notices and shoots at another stranger. Undisturbed by his narrow escape, Escamillo explains that he has taken a detour, while rounding up bulls for his next fight, to look for a gipsy he loves, named Carmen (this to a melodic line that recalls Carmen's motif). As a solo violin ironically comments, Escamillo smoothly announces that Carmen no longer loves the soldier who deserted her for her. Furious, José would kill the messenger bearing bad news, and Escamillo agrees to a knife duel. Because their duet is written in conventional form, the section in which they sing together (which contains some of the weakest music in the opera) returns for an obligatory second presentation. Although one half of the duet is frequently omitted, to judge the moral calibre of the two protagonists we need to see Escamillo, a killer of bulls and not of men, spare José, and then see José prepared without compunction to kill his rival during the second round. A jealousy that is now obsessive has deprived José of any self-restraint. Before, his actions were impulsive and passionate; now, there is a cruel intention in his anger. He is clearly capable of murder to keep possession of the woman for whom he has given up everything. Carmen intervenes, however, and Escamillo thanks her in smooth, modulating lines, offers José another match later on, and suavely carries out his original purpose of inviting Carmen to attend his next bullfight. He leaves at a leisurely pace to his refrain ([17] in D-flat major), smugly varied with new counterpoint and a scoring of divided cellos and woodwind.

Before the impatient smugglers can move on, Micaela is discovered. Once again a messenger from José's mother, she sings to earlier music [11] but this time José is not so receptive to his mother's wishes. When Carmen urges him to go, José refuses and, to blaring trombone accents, threatens her in a most powerful outburst [32], first in G-flat major, then a semi-tone higher; he swears to force her to accept the destiny that will join their lives until death. Micaela then reveals that José's mother is dying and wishes to pardon him at the last. Although José is shaken, he warns Carmen that he will find her again, and the fate motif [3a] sounds twice, loudly and ominously in French horns and woodwind. Just as José starts to leave, dragging Micaela, Escamillo is

Jusseaume's set for the final act at the Opera Comique in 1903 (Royal Opera House Archives)

heard off-stage, singing his refrain [17]. The toreador seems to be strolling off with Carmen's love, and she moves to join him. José menacingly blocks her way. The futile gesture brings down the curtain and prefigures the stage action in Act Four, where, with another off-stage presentation of [17], José carries out the threat of this gesture. (The parallelism of the two scenes was added late in rehearsal.) Music from the smugglers' chorus closes the finale. The dramatic power of this piece, the only one involving all four protagonists, derives partly from the quick succession of *coups de théâtre*: within the space of a few minutes Don José's world disintegrates before him as he loses his mother to death and Carmen to a rival. But it is Bizet's score that makes these moments unforgettable. Here the musical styles of the characters are heightened and play against one another to maximum effect; and the desperate urgency of José's threats are in some ways the emotional climax of the entire opera.

The brief final act is introduced by an *entr'acte* of picturesque scoring based on an Andalusian tune by Manuel Garcia [33]. As in Spanish folk tradition, the number pivots about the dominant and ends on this chord, which then binds the *entr'acte* to the opening chorus. We return to Seville and the daytime, to more of the routines of that city: the open-air market and the bullfight. The light-hearted activity of the crowded opening scenes sets off the tragic and lonely confrontation of the two protagonists. Energetic string parts illustrate the bustling market place and displaced rhythms (as the cries of the vendors start up), the confusion. A lengthy closing section in the orchestra fades into the Act's only dialogue scene. Frasquita and Mercedes advise us that Escamillo and Carmen are now together, and Zuniga mentions that José has escaped capture by the military authorities. The approaching parade builds up in the woodwind over a sustained low-E pedal note to snatches of the refrain theme [1]. As the crowd greets the matador and his assistants, they sing counterpoint to the music first heard in the *Prélude* [1], a refrain which alternates with sections describing each of the groups (the Alguazils [2], the Chulos and Banderilleros, the Picadors, and finally Escamillo [17]).

A brief but telling intimate scene between Escamillo and Carmen (only a quatrain of poetry) allows us to evaluate the dynamics of their relationship. Escamillo declares his love first [34], in suave lines reminiscent of his last appearance. (Carmen's potent love has not changed him.) She continues in the same vein (how unlike the stormy and/or manipulative scenes with José), and the harmony of their undemanding relationship is thus caught in the music. The bullfighters then enter the ring. In another brilliantly concise scene (six lines of poetry), Frasquita and Mercedes warn Carmen that José is hiding in the crowd. A graceful, four-bar melody, scored for flutes in thirds with bassoons moving in contrary motion, is repeated again and again while a cornet concealed in the orchestral texture suggests the lurking danger. Carmen, courageous, obstinate and fatalistic, makes no attempt to leave while everyone else, to a shortened version of the refrain [1], enters the bullring. Bizet adds an ominous, chromatic descending motif in the strings as José appears, and Carmen's own theme mutters low in the strings [3b], as at the end of the Card Trio.

The final duet is the masterpiece of the opera and one of the greatest closing scenes in all opera. All that goes before is a preparation for this confrontation, whose genius lies in its emotional logic and concise dramatic structure. The piece may be divided into three sections, each corresponding to an increasingly heightened emotional level. It begins quietly with a few tense words in recitative, coldly delivered. José offers to forget the past and start over again elsewhere; Carmen's firm refusal elicits the supplicating lines (over throbbing

Placido Domingo and Shirley Verrett at Covent Garden (photo: Reg Wilson)

rhythms reminiscent of the Flower Song) that are repeated as a duet where they sing at cross purposes. The second section opens with José's emotional realization of something his reason has already told him — that he cannot salvage their love. A low clarinet over timpani first expresses his anxiety. Then dissonant chords illustrate his despair as he sings *'Tu ne m'aimes donc plus'*, first as a question, then as an exclamation culminating in a G-major chord. Carmen's unemotional, *'Non, je ne t'aimes plus'*, produces a steel-edged, passionate response [37]. Rapid triplets underscore José's vehement agitation and strings reinforce the melody at pitch and at the octave to strengthen the emotional intensity of the passage. Carmen is unmoved before the implicit threat and swears, in another jagged and demanding vocal line, to live and die free. The third and climactic section of the duet is interspersed with backstage choral outbursts. Their closed, regular phrasing provides a striking contrast with the angry, broken phrases of the soloists. Twice Carmen attempts to leave [1], and she goads José with her brutal honesty, by proclaiming even before death that she now loves Escamillo. While José makes his final threats, [3a] sounds four times in the full orchestra. Fanfares proclaim Escamillo's victory, and Carmen, at last furious herself, throws down a ring that José had given her, rejecting any last shred of connection with him. He screams, *'Eh bien, damnée!'* to a high F# and stabs her as Escamillo is acclaimed by the populace (to [17] in F# major).* It had long been conventional in *opéra-comique* to include a joyful chorus at the end, but not off-stage, and not transformed by the situation into a supremely ironic counterpart to the stage action. To the familiar refrain Bizet adds a simple countermelody in the orchestra which amply comments on the tragic situation. José makes no

35

attempt to escape. The crowd, leaving the bullring, discovers him kneeling by her body. He sings only to a single note as the fate motif sounds, and then rises to a last possessive and passionate outburst on *'ma Carmen adorée'*.

The curtain falls immediately, for the tragedy is complete: Carmen dead, José doomed. Not merely a convincing portrait of a soldier's moral disintegration and a gipsy's murder, *Carmen* reaches the level of genuine tragedy in its representation of an all-consuming passion that develops into jealous obsession. The story of José, a proud man torn apart by guilt (after he has forsaken his duty to his mother, to his society) and infatuation arouses our pity, but it is Bizet's music that magnifies the central characters to the level of archetypes and vividly represents the emotional forces that buffet them. With his master touch, Carmen becomes virtually a force of nature, igniting men's desire; and José becomes all those who love totally and are destroyed by this vulnerability.

Bizet explores the limits of a musician's resources. He employs conventional music or forms when appropriate and stretches and abandons this idiom when the drama no longer fits the old moulds. His score teems with melodic invention, striking orchestration, and daring modulation, which satisfy on a purely musical level but always serve a dramatic purpose. Most importantly, the restraint and conciseness he achieved after paring down and rewriting have produced a very French masterpiece, of expert pacing, a sustained inspiration of idea, and an exquisite balance of music and drama that is the aim of all opera but attained by only the few.

* At this point, Oeser restores descending chromatic scales and stage directions specifying that Carmen should fall and die *before* Escamillo's refrain begins. Bizet, quite rightly, rejected this version in favour of the immediate and powerfully ironic impact of Carmen's death during her new lover's signature tune. For more on the problems of the Oeser edition, see Winton Dean, 'The True *Carmen?*' *Musical Times* 1965, pp. 846-855.

A print of the final scene in the 1875 Paris production (Raymond Mander and Joe Mitchenson Theatre Collection)

'Carmen': A tragedy of love, sun and death

Michel Rabaud

And really, I have appeared to myself, every time I have heard *Carmen*, to be more of a philosopher, a better philosopher than at other times: I have become so patient, so happy, so Indian, so *sedate* . . . Five hours sitting: the first stage of holiness! . . . This music seems to me to be perfect. It approaches lightly, nimbly, and with courtesy. It is amiable, it does not produce *sweat*. 'What is good is easy; everything divine runs with light feet': – the first proposition of my æsthetics. This music is wicked, subtle, and fatalistic; it remains popular at the same time . . . It is rich. It is precise. It builds, it organises, it completes; it is thus the antithesis to the polypus in music, 'infinite melody'.

This enthusiastic appraisal of Bizet's masterpiece by Friedrich Nietzsche in *The Wagner Case* (1888) is usually regarded with suspicion, even by Bizet's devotees. It is common to consider that Nietzsche was carried away by his wrath towards his former idol, that challenging Wagner with Bizet cannot be taken seriously – indeed for Wagnerites, such an idea is madness. Poor, charming and unpretentious Bizet did not deserve such an embarrassing supporter.

The story is well-known: in his years of collaboration with Wagner, Nietzsche drew up a theory of modern musical drama, derived from a renewed interest in ancient Greek myth and tragedy, which Wagner was to fulfill in his operas. It implied for him a total rejection of Christianity, metaphysical psychology and sentimental romanticism — all of which he eventually realised were still at the root of Wagner's world, and which he described as modern decadence. As the antithesis of Wagnerian drama, the true essence of tragedy lay for Nietzsche in paganism, irrationality, reality and sensuality. It required concision and clarity, rhythm and dance, and a full alliance of gaiety and fatalism — sunshine and blood. All these were necessary for the Dionysiac 'art of the future' he was calling for, an art which would whole-heartedly assent to passion and life, instead of rejecting them, as in the Christian tradition he execrated. To achieve that, one should get away from the gloomy idealism and gluey sentimentality which prevailed in Germany, and look towards the South: '*il faut méditerraniser la musique*' became one of his mottoes.

There are stunning similarities between these views and Bizet's own conceptions, which he exposed particularly in his letters to his disciple Edmond Galabert; letters Nietzsche could not have read, but which seem totally to validate his analysis of *Carmen*. Bizet described himself as a 'pagan', and rejected Christianity ('religion is a policeman', he wrote) to the point that, as opposed to most composers of his time, he could not, after his early *Te Deum*, set himself down to writing any other religious work. After eager investigations in philosophy, and some hesitations, he finally discarded all systems. Philosophy is incompatible with good art: 'with philosophy, you will make some Ary Scheffer or Paul Delaroche, but I defy you to make any Giorgione or Veronese, or even Salvator Rosa'. He was particularly infuriated by the idea that art should progress in parallel with science. On the contrary, 'the more reason advances, the more art falls to pieces'. He also repeatedly

Medea Mei-Figner as Carmen (Stuart-Liff Collection)

Georges Baklanoff, the Russian baritone, as Don José (Royal Opera House Archives)

campaigned against sentimentality, in which he accused Galabert of indulging: 'I abhor this hotch-potch of vice, sentimentality, philosophy and genius which produces a Rousseau' . . . which was echoed later by Nietzsche, in *Twilight of the Idols* (1889): 'Rousseau, the first modern man, an idealist and scoundrel in one person'. This determined attitude sets Bizet apart from most of his contemporaries.

Thus musical inspiration cannot be rooted in religious, philosophical or sentimental considerations: on the contrary, Bizet encouraged a direct approach to the passion, sensuality and reality of life. This is clearly shown in his recommendation to Galabert: 'Plunge forward, try and attain pathos, avoid dryness, do not neglect sensuality, you austere philosopher! Think of Mozart and read him assiduously. Keep by your side *Don Giovanni*, the *Nozze*, the *Flute* and *Così fan tutte*. Read Weber also. *Vive le soleil et l'amour* . . . Don't laugh at me nor send me to hell: this can be a way to a very exalting sort of philosophy. Art has its demands . . .' Mozart, Weber, sensual love and sunlight: these seem the best ways to approach *Carmen*.

Indeed, after the failure of his opera *Djamileh*, Bizet turns south. Provence attracts him first. But he keeps far away from the gentle local colour of Gounod's *Mireille*, and innovates in *L'Arlésienne* a combination of folk musical material and intense lyricism, obtaining a poignant effect from the sharp and often unresolved contrast between the two levels. 'I am absolutely certain', he then writes, 'that I have found my way: I know what I am doing.' His next project would have been a grand opera on *El Cid* by Guillen de Castro — and *not* on the famous play by Corneille — 'in its true Spanish colour', as Bizet himself pointed out. Passion and death under a sun far more implacable than that of Provence. He never completed it, but meanwhile wrote *Carmen*, which he saw as 'a *gay* thing I will try to treat as *tightly* as possible'. This gaiety clearly has nothing to do with light entertainment, although unfortunately that is how it is often staged. It is instead close to what Nietzsche defines as 'Dionysiac' jubilation. Hot blood, provocative insolence, cruel irony, gambling with death: this is the 'true Spanish colour' Bizet achieved from the explosive energy of the first bars — so remote from the mysterious, insinuating opening of *Tristan* — to the incredible tension and abrupt violence of the last act, where the strange 'blood wedding' — to use Lorca's words — of Carmen and Don José is set against that of the bull and the matador.

One of the structural features of the opera, which did not appear in Mérimée's short story and which accounts for a number of transformations in the libretto, is the defeat of sentimental love by a vital passion. Rather than the weak soldier who renounces his duties to follow a dangerous seducer (which is how he too often appears), Bizet's Don José is a man whose fatal vocation compels him to abandon a pale sentimental love and banal occupations, and to plunge into what he does not know — the outlaw world of passion. Like Des Grieux when meeting Manon in Prévost's novel, Don José begins to live when he meets Carmen: love acts as a second birth, transforming a rather ectoplasmic character into a full-blooded man. One could argue that if he shows weakness it is not by following Carmen, but by being unable to follow her completely. He returns to his dying mother instead of responding to Carmen's vital challenge: he is not a free man and he loses her.

Because of this, the introduction of Micaela into the opera becomes a

Marie Charbonnel as
Carmen
(Stuart-Liff Collection)

Alma Gluck as Micaela

necessity. She represents Christianity, family bonds, legality and sentimental love, all to be broken down by the irruption of passion. She shares with Don José a musical vocabulary of tender and intense lyricism, which is utterly antithetic to Carmen's songs and dances. Throughout his score, Bizet makes a masterly use of this contrast. In their First Act duet, Don José and Micaela immediately find a common musical language to evoke sweet feelings about their engagement and his beloved mother, which develops into a formal duet. In the Act Two duet between Don José and Carmen, on the other hand, the dramatic discrepancy between Don José's lyrical register in his aria '*La fleur que tu m'avais jetée*' and Carmen's tarentella rhythm in '*Là-bas dans la montagne*' does not allow them to go into a properly balanced duet. It is made obvious, by purely musical means, that they neither speak the same language, nor share the same values. In the course of Acts Three and Four, Don José's lyricism loses all its gentleness and becomes imperious, tense and open to

40

outbursts of extreme violence, showing the evolution of the character. This use of stylistic contrasts as a dramatic compositional procedure seems quite particular to Bizet: Wagner avoided it, and few later composers achieved it as brilliantly as Bizet.

The character of Escamillo is the other main addition in the opera to Mérimée's story. He is an incarnation of sheer virility, and Bizet reveals this otherwise subdued aspect of Don José's character by giving the two men a carefully balanced quarelling duet: by eventually defeating the toreador, Don José displays the seriousness of his passion and his skill as a fighter. But although Carmen leaves Don José for Escamillo, it does not follow that the two men are rivals of comparable stature. Escamillo's love is gallantry of a kind similar to that which Carmen lightheartedly rebuked in Zuniga. He is ready to wait for his turn in Carmen's favours, without showing too much impatience. The quality of their relationship appears from the very abbreviated and underplayed duet they have in the final Act: they sign a superficial and quick engagement of love, in music which has a Mozartian flavour, perhaps reminiscent of Zerlina's aria '*Batti, batti*' in *Don Giovanni*. If he appeals to Carmen, despite his shallow vanity, it is because he is on familiar terms with death: the first thing he offers her is 'to pronounce her name the next time he kills a bull'. He freely risks his life with every bull he fights, and freedom is indeed her strongest passion.

The enduring mystery and fascination of Carmen is due to the fact that we are never given the least psychological clue to the deep motives of her actions and the hierarchy of her feelings. She does not comment on herself: she only states repeatedly her unyielding will to remain free. Does she love Don José? She never says so, otherwise than elusively and playfully, and she never attempts, as Massenet's Manon constantly does, to give reasons for her behaviour. Nevertheless, she does choose him, by throwing him a flower in the First Act, presumably because he *is* different from other men: he alone does not even look at her. The music which immediately precedes her gesture, her 'fate' theme ending on a long silence after a suspended single note, obviously refuses to comment on her feelings — Fate has made its entrance, sudden and unexplained. She is disappointed several times by Don José's indecisiveness, and mocks him sharply. But she is intrigued by a man for whom love is not a game, and who is so deadly serious about it. Indeed it is death she finally challenges by accepting, despite all warnings, to meet Don José. And she also knows it is worth missing the *fiesta*, over which she was to reign, in order to have this confrontation.

Such a provocative attitude is not disguised suicide, nor an idealistic attempt to sublimate her love, but something rationally absurd she simply *has* to do to remain herself. In this respect, Carmen's death is radically different from that of Isolde whose radiant joy in death comes from her mystical belief that eternal love will transcend it. Both she and Tristan are conceived as passive *victims* of love and death, whereas Carmen and Don José act their love and death until the end. By killing her — and not Escamillo, which would seem at first glance more rational — Don José fulfils a need to possess her. By confronting him with courage, Carmen proclaims her free will and firmly asserts her ego; she *deliberately* chooses to accomplish her destiny. This is what Nietzsche considered essentially tragic: to face death not in an idealistic *refusal* of life, but in a full, if paradoxical, *assent* to it.

A truly Dionysiac interpretation of life is singing, dancing and irrational gaiety. This is exemplified by the type of music Bizet has given not only to Carmen and Escamillo, but also to one of the main protagonists of the opera — the crowd, in its various aspects. The score contains far more ensembles and

Rosa Ponselle: the four acts of 'Carmen' (Ida Cook Collection)

choruses than arias and duets. The function of the chorus is not to express a particular patriotic, military or religious idea — as in Verdi or in Mussorgsky, for instance — but to give voice to joy and freedom in everyday life. Official values and authority are often the butt of this popular voice, from the children's acid and ironical commentary on the pompous changing of the guards to their booing of the 'ugly faced' alguaziles in the last Act, from the women insolently singing of their pleasure in smoking to the smugglers complacently asking for assistance in 'any dirty work'. There is more than a flavour of anarchist immorality in all this, which did not fail to horrify the first audiences.

There are many benefits from Bizet's choice of dance rythms and song tunes. Firstly, it sets, throughout the opera, that incessant motion and fast pace of life which allows very little time for reflection or lyrical development: the few arias in the score (apart from Micaela's) are rather short. It also excludes any possibility of musical commentary. Contrary to Wagner's idea that 'drama is the end, music only the means', music in Bizet's work never renounces its autonomy. This accounts for Bizet's acceptance of the classical features of the *opéra-comique* genre, which allowed clarity to the musical discourse. 'Be clear' was one of his favourite mottoes, and he was irritated by the frequent reproach of Wagnerism that superficial critics would make of his

Kenneth Neate and Edith Coates who sang in English in 1947 at Covent Garden (the first production by the Covent Garden Opera Company after the war). Edith Coates was also a celebrated Carmen at Sadler's Wells. (Royal Opera House Archives)

music. He greatly admired the 'Olympian greatness and inspiration' he found in Wagner: 'the bourgeois and the musical snobs,' he said 'realize they are dealing with a great fellow, and they flounder'. But he also criticized in *Rienzi*, which is certainly not a masterpiece, 'bizarre and bad style; music of decadence rather than of the future — some parts detestable, some admirable!' According to Bizet, music does not have to mimic the external or interior action, nor submit to the words of the text, nor even express the composer's feelings about the drama, but it must, on the other hand, avoid mere ornamentation.

Bizet's original solution to the old problem of matching music and drama, symphony and declamation, is to create a *tension* between the action and the musical discourse, and not to aim at a *fusion* of the two. This tension is achieved by various means, such as ellipse, understatement, apparent irrelevance of the action, ironical discrepancy or deliberate contrast between the two. Many examples such as Carmen's insolent song when she eludes Zuniga's questions, spring immediately to mind; but also, less obviously, the light and unconcerned *ritournelle* running under the dramatic dialogue of Act Four in which Carmen is warned that she is in danger; the surprising major chord which punctuates the cruel discovery by Don José that Carmen no longer loves him; or the striking ellipse in the musical treatment of her

Tatiana Troyanos as Carmen at Covent Garden (photo: Donald Southern)

stabbing, a simple line overwhelmed by the boisterous joy of the off-stage chorus.

The music therefore does not *contain* the drama, but helps to *stage* it in its full tragic relief. It is said that once, during a performance of one of his operas, Wagner put his hands over the eyes of a woman who was eagerly looking at the stage, saying 'Don't watch, listen'. This is not to be recommended with *Carmen*. It demands to be seen, inasmuch as it has the deadly appeal of a bull-fight, and loses more than any other opera from being only heard on record. The non-committal attitude of a composer who avoids imposing or even suggesting any point of view, leaves much to the imagination of the interpreters and the audience. As a result of this theatrical appeal, *Carmen* is probably the most often performed opera of the whole repertoire.

Brahms, who as a professional musician might have been expected to prefer studying the score, went to twenty performances of *Carmen* in 1875, and several times again in 1893, accompanied by the young Debussy. Neither would Nietzsche have missed a single performance of an opera which, before irremediably collapsing into deep mental night, he beautifully defined as a perfect tragedy of human love:

> Love put back into nature . . . Love as *Fate*, *fatality*, cynical, innocent, cruel love — and thus true to *nature* . . . Love in its ways is the war of the sexes, its basis their *mortal hatred*. I do not know any other instance where tragic humour, which constitutes the essence of love, is expressed more absolutely, in a more shattering phrase, than in Don José's last words:
>
> > *C'est moi qui l'ai tuée, ma Carmen,*
> > *Ma Carmen adorée!*

Bizet and His Text

Nell and John Moody

Carmen has so often in performance seemed not quite to reach the expectations promised by score and libretto, appearing to be a rather inadequate 'Grand Opera' with banal recitative, about a tough femme-fatale gipsy and a rather pathetic corporal. About 1965 with a production date pencilled, we needed to find out all we could about Bizet's original intentions and how they could be restored. The authorities made it quite clear how first and foremost he never intended *Carmen* to be played as Grand Opera. In his own words, to his friend Guiraud, 'Your place is at the Opéra. I am afraid of not having the necessary fullness. I shall shine at the Opéra Comique; I shall enlarge and transform the genre.' He had already chosen Mérimée's story as leading in the real direction he wanted to go. Instead of the set pieces of Grand Opera he desired the variety and Dionysiac vitality of real life. That was his gift. As Nietzsche summed it up — 'Have more moving, more tragic utterances ever been heard on stage? And how have they been obtained? . . . Without falseness of any kind: free from the lie of the grand style.'

At the first performance in March 1875, after very stormy rehearsals, his intentions were to a great extent realised. But he died on June 5, and the production disappeared within a year. By September 1875 it was being prepared in Vienna with recitatives by Guiraud. The tradition of *Carmen* as Grand Opera had already begun.

To get back to Bizet's original conception a new translation was needed which would restore the spirit of Mérimée — his vivid images, and direct simplicity of language. The English had to have a unity of style in lyrics and dialogue. It had to be flexible enough to be sung or spoken very easily and to move with clarity in great variations of rhythm and speed. The stresses that correspond with the musical movement — the 'footfall' as Ernest Ansermet called it — of the words, must be more than ordinarily exact and easy because of the *élan* of the music. All this would affect every single performer, onstage and in the pit. So we started with the Quintet as a test; after about twenty versions we began to feel we were getting nearer the style.

Like Walther Felsenstein in his famous 1949 production conducted by Klemperer at the Komische Oper in East Berlin, we felt that the clue to Bizet's new method was in dovetailing the spoken word and music into an exciting texture of sound, by the use of dialogue over music (*Mélodrame*). Although this had been done before, Bizet's use of it is far more fundamental than would appear at first sight. This method does not lengthen the opera because the time taken for the dialogue without the music would be the same. But it heightens the tension. For example:

> The *mélodrame* for Morales and Don José, during the changing of the guard in Act One, has a little tune which suggests Don José's old world background. This dialogue, together with the commands for changing sentries, times exactly with the music, as Bizet planned.
> The scene between Carmen and Don José before she throws the flower.
> Zuniga with Carmen: her tra-la-la song as her hands are tied.

45

Regina Resnik as Carmen (Stuart-Liff Collection)

Rosa Olitzka as Carmen (Stuart-Liff Collection)

Act Two. Zuniga and the Girls, over the off-stage chorus before the arrival of Escamillo.

The Smugglers over the two verses of José's 'Alcala' song.

Even more important, because it is used all through the opera, is the logical extension of this technique — starting the dialogue over the end of a musical number and starting into the music before the dialogue has finished. Apart from shortening the length of the opera and discouraging unnecessarily distracting applause, Bizet in this way minimised the jolt for both audience and singers between spoken and sung sections, and achieved the unity and dramatic excitement on which so much depends.

Again breaking with tradition, in some highly dramatic scenes he swept the conventional lyrics into an heroic, almost ritual, quasi-recitative. For instance:

Carmen's dance, and the scene from the bugle entry up to the Flower song in Act Two.

Escamillo and José's duel in Act Three.

In Act Four, the scene in which the girls warn Carmen that Don José is near (which is almost *mélodrame* although it is written out in notation).

The tremendous last scene.

An awareness of the new technique Bizet was using is vital to a successful performance of *Carmen*, and it must be carried through with Gallic lightness and speed (which means enough rehearsal time!).*

The Italian Bruna Castagna, a famous Carmen at the Met. between 1936 and 1945.

Conchita Supervia as Carmen at Covent Garden in 1935 (Royal Opera House Archives)

The librettists, in cutting Mérimée's novel to opera length had to leave out much illuminating detail. This, followed later by careless translations and drastic cutting of the published dialogue, has often made definition of the characters in the opera inadequate and in fact downright wrong. Both Carmen and Don José have often suffered from this.

As is so clear from Mérimée, they are a pair of absolute opposites, fatally attractive to each other. To José, Carmen has all the things he lacks: a total lack of inhibition, irresponsibility in personal relationships and an infinite capacity for enjoying life. To her, José is equally fascinating: a gentleman, with looks, and an elegant detachment, who does not chase every girl who comes his

* In fact if this dovetailing is skilfully done we have proved in performance that the complete opera (including two 20 minute intervals and a quick change between Acts Three and Four of 3 minutes) can be played in 3½ hours cutting no more than 100 bars of the Urchins, 70 bars of the Cuadrilla, about 80 bars unnecessary in a smaller theatre for entrances and exits, and cutting only 25% of the full dialogue. Act Two, for instance, plays only 44 minutes without cuts, if the *mélodrame* is carefully handled. According to the note of timings made at the Opéra Comique dress rehearsal in 1875, even without the 70 bars cut by Bizet (i.e. 1½ minutes of music), Act Two played 7 minutes longer. No doubt the composer concluded that the only way to maintain the excitement in his opera, when faced with an uncooperative production, was to postpone his experiments at *mélodrame*. As an experienced man of the theatre, Bizet was certainly aware of the practical difficulties of obtaining the results he wanted. It is rewarding to see how well his intentions can be carried out today.

Blanche Thebom as Carmen (photo: Bender)

way, yet is an obviously passionate, if rather buttoned-up, young man, whom it would be a pleasure to unbutton.

According to the book, to which the operatic characterisation is faithful, Carmen was small, slim, young, 'prettier than any gipsy', with eyes that had a sensual yet savage look with a wolfish glint. She wore her clothes beautifully and was a professional dancer at parties. Because she could not afford scent, she wore heavily scented flowers, acacia in the day and jasmine by night. She 'munched sweets like a child of six', was always laughing, sending people up, with a lovely sense of the ridiculous; yet able to cope with any situation. She was more than faithful to her own people. She obeyed gipsy law: she paid her debts — to José in kind for freeing her from prison. José exasperated her by his possessiveness — 'dog and wolf don't mate for long' . . . 'I must be *free* to do as I like', but when he was wounded or ill she would nurse him night and day devotedly. At the end she goes to him deliberately, knowing he may kill her, yet she will not surrender to him: she must be free. Basically a really heroic character.

José is a proud Basque gentleman, a Don of a very old family; stalwart, good-looking, and of a very passionate nature although inhibited by his upbringing. He was being trained, in the family tradition, to go into the Church. But his studies came second to his love of sport. One day after a game of Pelota, his opponent picked a quarrel with him. José's terrific temper suddenly blazed, the boy was killed, José had to leave the country. He joined

Bernardo de Muro as Don José (Stuart-Liff Collection)

Sigrid Arnoldson as Carmen (Stuart-Liff Collection)

the army as a ranker and soon became a corporal. On three other occasions in the opera we see his temper blaze. In Act Two, when his officer slaps his face, he would have killed him; in Act Three when he fights Escamillo; and at the end, when Carmen throws his ring at him, it suddenly blazes again and he has killed her before he knows what he has done.

Subconsciously he can never escape from his family morality; his duty as a son, as a soldier, his feeling that marriage must be for life. When he returns to the bullring in the last scene to find Carmen, his only instinct is to 'save' her, to take her away to start a new life. Both are heroic in their different ways: in spite of the degradation José has suffered through Carmen, his love for her is as strong as ever. The tragedy is that they should ever have met.

Micaela, often played as a nonentity, was Halévy's invention, thought up to sweeten the 'disgusting' Carmen pill for the disapproving management. But the text, and Bizet's treatment of it, created a rounded character. She was brought up by José's mother, as a daughter of a good family, fit to marry the son and heir. She has a strength that can challenge Carmen, and a wit that can deal with soldiery or smugglers.

There is much else in Mérimée's novel[†] about the characters which can help us to understand them. It is compulsive reading. No wonder Bizet wanted to set it!

[†] All Mérimée's quotations are taken from 'Carmen and Colomba' translated by Eric Sutton.

Mary Garden as Carmen (Royal College of Music)

Thematic Guide

Many of the themes from the opera have been identified in the articles by numbers in square brackets, which refer to the themes set out on these pages. The themes are also identified by the numbers in brackets at the corresponding points in the libretto, so that the words can be related to the musical themes.

[1] *Prélude*
Allegro giocoso

[2]
Allegro giocoso

[3a] *Carmen's Fate*
Andante moderato
tutta forza

[3b]
Allegro moderato

[4] **CHORUS**
Allegretto moderato / *légèrement*
All a - round here, peo - ple won - der, Peo - ple come, peo - ple go;
Sur la pla - ce, cha - cun pas - se, Cha - cun vient, cha - cun va;

[5] **MORALES**
Allegretto mosso / *Léger, mais bien rhythmé*
He will be here the mo - ment that the new guard
Il y se - ra Quand la gar - de mon - tan - te

[6] *No. 2 March of the Urchins*
Allegretto moderato

[7] CHORUS OF CIGARETTE GIRLS

Andantino

Our eyes fol - low gent - ly where smoke is curl - ing,
Dans __ l'air nous sui - vons des yeux La fu - mé - e,

[8] CARMEN *No. 4 Habañera*

Allegretto, quasi andantino

Love's a bird that will live in free - dom, That no man
L'a - mour est un oi - seau re - bel - le Que nul ne

ev - er learned to tame,
peut __ ap - pri - voi - ser.

[9] CARMEN

Allegretto, quasi andantino

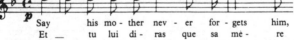

Oh love was born to gip - sy life,
L'a - mour est en - fant de Bo - hême,

[10] MICAELA (*from No. 6 Duet*)

Andantino quasi Allegretto / *simplement*

I've come in - stead of her, with something that she gave me, Here's a let - ter.
J'ap - por - te de sa part, fi - dè - le mes - sa - gè - re, Cet - te let - tre.

[11] MICAELA

Allegro moderato *espressivo*

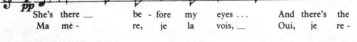

Say his mo - ther nev - er for - gets him,
Et __ tu lui di - ras que sa mè - re

[12] JOSE

Andantino moderato

She's there __ be - fore my eyes ... And there's the
Ma mè - re, je la vois, __ Oui, je re -

vil - lage house I re - mem - ber!
vois __ mon vil - la - ge!

[13] CARMEN / *No. 8 Chanson*

Allegretto molto moderato

Tra la la la la la la la! You may beat me or
Tra la la la la la la, Cou - pe - moi, brû - le -

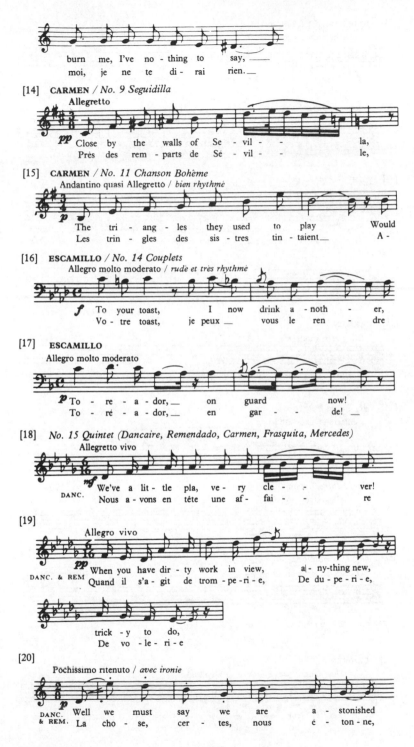

burn me, I've no - thing to say, \
moi, je ne te di - rai rien.

[14] **CARMEN** / *No. 9 Seguidilla*

Allegretto

pp Close by the walls of Se - vil - - la, \
Près des rem - parts de Sé - vil - - le,

[15] **CARMEN** / *No. 11 Chanson Bohème*

Andantino quasi Allegretto / *bien rhythmé*

p The tri - ang - les they used to play Would \
Les trin - gles des sis - tres tin - taient A -

[16] **ESCAMILLO** / *No. 14 Couplets*

Allegro molto moderato / *rude et très rhythmé*

f To your toast, I now drink a - noth - er, \
Vo - tre toast, je peux vous le ren - dre

[17] **ESCAMILLO**

Allegro molto moderato

p To - re - a - dor, on guard now! \
To - ré - a - dor, en gar - de!

[18] *No. 15 Quintet (Dancaire, Remendado, Carmen, Frasquita, Mercedes)*

Allegretto vivo

mf
DANC. We've a lit - tle pla, ve - ry cle - - ver! \
Nous a - vons en tête une af - fai - - re

[19]

Allegro vivo

pp
DANC. & REM When you have dir - ty work in view, a| - ny-thing new, \
Quand il s'a - git de trom - pe - ri - e, De du - pe - ri - e,

trick - y to do, \
De vo - le - ri - e

[20]

Pochissimo ritenuto / *avec ironie*

p
DANC. Well we must say we are a - stonished \
& REM. La cho - se, cer - tes, nous é - ton - ne,

53

[21] JOSE / *No. 15 Chanson*

Allegretto moderato

"Hey, ho - la!   Who goes there?" "Friend from Al - ca - la!"
Hal - te là!   Qui va · là? Dra - gon d'Al - ca - la! __

[22] *Carmen's Dance*

Allegretto moderato

La _____ la __ la ____ la __   la _____ la _ la ____ la __

[23] JOSE / *Flower Song*

Andantino / *con amore*

Here   is   the flow - er that you threw   me,   While
La   fleur que   tu m'a - vais je - té -   e,   Dans

in   the jail it nev - er left me · __
ma pri - son __   m'é - tait res - té - e,

[24] CARMEN

Allegretto moderato

In - to the hills where none would find   you,
Là - bas, là - bas dans la mon - ta -   gne,

[25] *Act Three Entr'acte*

Allegretto, quasi Andantino

[26] *No 18 Introduction*

Allegretto moderato

[27] *No. 19 Trio (Frasquita, Mercedes, Carmen)*

Allegretto con moto / *con grazia*

FRASQ. So there we   are,   now say   my   beau - ties,
& MERC. Et main - te - nant, par - lez, __ mes __ bel - les,

[28] CARMEN

Andantino / *très également et simplement*

You nev - er can es - cape their un - re - len - ting
En   vain pour é - vi - ter les ré - pon - ses a -

an - swer, How - e - ver hard you try!
mèr - es, En vain tu mè - le - ras, ____

[29] **FRASQUITA, MERCEDES** / *No. 20 Ensemble*

Allegretto

mf

Leave our three guards, for us to deal with!
Quant au doua - nier, c'est notre af - fai - re!

[30] **MICAELA** *No. 21 Air*

Andante molto

p

I said there was no - thing could scare me,
Je dis, ____ que rien ne m'é - pou - van - te.

[31] **MICAELA**

Allegro molto moderato

mf

I shall meet that crea - ture at last
Je vais voir de près ____ cet - te fem - me

[32] **JOSE**

Moderato / *resolument*

f

For me death be - fore I leave ____ you
Dût - il m'en coû - ter la vi - e.

[33] *Act Three Entr'acte*

Allegro vivo

pp

[34] **ESCAMILLO**

Andantino / *espressivo*

p

If you love me, Car - men, __ if you love me, Car - men, __
Si tu m'ai - mes, Car - men, __ si tu m'ai - mes, Car - men, __

[35] **JOSE**

Allegro moderato / *avec passion*

mf

But I still love you, more than ev - er.
Mais moi, Car - men, je t'aime en - co - - re

Bibliography

One of the best studies of any composer is Winton Dean's *Georges Bizet: His Life and Work* (Dent, 1975) in which a witty and perceptive biography, packed with illuminating detail, is combined with assessments and descriptions of the music. Winton Dean is also the author of a number of important articles which have marked the history of the opera in the last 35 years. Mina Curtiss's *Bizet and his World* (New York, 1958 and London, 1959) is still an excellent alternative source. Martin Cooper has written the classic general survey *A History of French Music from the Death of Berlioz to the Death of Fauré* (London, 1951) as well as *Georges Bizet* (London, 1938) and *Carmen* (London, 1947).

Prosper Mérimée's novel has been republished, in French, with an introduction by N.S. Wilson (Harrap, 1962) and, in English, (edited by M. Tilby, Harrap 1981). An earlier translation is that by Eric Sutton, published by Hamish Hamilton on 1949. Nietzsche's essays *Der Fall Wagner* and *Götzen-Dammerung* are available in editions of his collected works and the latter is available as *Twilight of the Idols* in Penguin Classics, 1969 (trans. R.J. Hollingdale). Nietzsche's *The Wagner Case (Der Fall Wagner)* has been translated by Walter Kaufmann and republished by Vintage Books (1962) with *The Birth of Tragedy*. Penguin Classics also include a *Nietzsche Reader* (1977) and *Ecce Homo* (1979). Bizet's own letters are, unfortunately, not readily available and have not been translated: *Lettres: Impressions de Rome 1857-60; La Commune 1870* (Paris 1908) and *Lettres à un ami 1867-72* (edited by Edmond Galabert (Paris, 1909)).

Contributors

Nicholas John is Editorial Co-ordinator for English National Opera and author of 'Opera' to be published in the *Topics in Music* series by Oxford University Press.

Martin Cooper, formerly music critic of *The Daily Telegraph*, is the author of *French Music (1870-1925)*, *Ideas and Music* and *Beethoven — The Last Decade*.

Lesley A. Wright is Visiting Assistant Professor of Music at Indiana State University and submitted a Dissertation on Bizet for her doctorate at Princeton.

Michel Rabaud is Lecturer in Literature at the French Institute in London, and has studied piano, composition and conducting.

Nell Moody, formerly a professional singer, is now a singing teacher at the Bristol Old Vic School and the Bath Academy at Corsham, and has translated several German plays. John Moody, actor and director, formerly Director of Productions and then Joint Artistic Director for Welsh National Opera, is now Counsellor to the board of WNO. Together they have translated numerous operas.

Carmen

Opera in Four Acts by Georges Bizet
Text by Henri Meilhac and Ludovic Halévy
after the novel by Prosper Mérimée
English version by Nell and John Moody

Carmen was first performed at the Opéra Comique, Paris, on March 3, 1875. The first performance in England was at Her Majesty's Theatre, London on June 22, 1878 (in Italian and with recitatives). The first performance in New York was (in Italian) on October 23, 1878, at The Academy of Music.

The Carl Rosa Company seem to have given the first performances in English, and with dialogue, on February 5, 1879. This was an adaptation, rather than a literal translation.

This translation was written for and first performed by Welsh National Opera at the New Theatre, Cardiff on September 25, 1967 in a production by the translators and using three-quarters of the dialogue.

Translators' Note

Bizet often found the hackneyed formula of foursquare verses and endless rhymes frustrated his dramatic needs, and had no hesitation in altering his librettists' text, adding, cutting, or transposing words, half or whole lines, etc. to give strength and variety to his final musical forms. In our translation we have followed Bizet in not being bound by formal rhymes at the expense of dramatic directness, sense and feeling.

The dialogue is translated in full, but those sections of it that are cut in the ENO production are marked with square brackets.

The proper names in the text are used in their Spanish rather than their French or Anglicised forms, to get some unity of accent.

The scene for Morales (a 'pantomime' concluding the first scene of Act One) has been relegated to the end of the text on page 125 because, although it appears in the 1875 piano-vocal score, it is rarely performed.

The longer stage directions, such as scene descriptions, are taken from the published French libretto; the shorter directions are supplemented by those in the 1875 vocal score.

THE CHARACTERS

Don José *a corporal (brigadier)*	*tenor*
Escamillo *a toreador*	*baritone*
Dancairo (Le Dancaïre) ⎫ *smugglers*	*tenor*
Remendado (Le Remendado) ⎭	*tenor*
Zuniga *a lieutenant*	*bass*
Morales (Moralès) *a corporal (brigadier)*	*baritone*
Lillas Pastia *an inn-keeper*	
Andres (Andrès) *another lieutenant*	*tenor*
A guide	
Carmen *a gipsy*	*soprano*
Micaela (Micaëla)	*soprano*
Frasquita ⎫ *friends of Carmen*	*soprano*
Mercedes (Mercédès) ⎭	*soprano*
An officer	

Soldiers, Cigarette Girls, Gipsies and Smugglers

Act One

A square in Seville. On the right, the door of the tobacco factory. At the back of the stage there is a bridge which can be crossed, spanning the whole width of the stage. Access to the bridge from the stage is by a curved staircase, which curves to the right above the tobacco factory door. There is an entrance from under the bridge. On the left, in the foreground, is the Guardroom. In front of the Guardroom there is a little covered balcony, with two or three steps up to it. In a rack, near the Guardroom, are the Dragoons' lances with their red and yellow pennants. When the curtain rises we see about fifteen soldiers (Dragoons of the Alcala regiment) grouped in front of the Guardroom. Some sit smoking, others lean on the balustrade. Passers-by in the square — people in a hurry, people on business, come and go, meet, greet, or jostle each other, etc..

Scene One. *Morales, Micaela, Soldiers, Passers-by. / No. 1. Introduction*

CHORUS
(soldiers of the guard on duty)

All around here,	[4]	Sur la place,
People wander,		Chacun passe,
People come, people go;		Chacun vient, chacun va;
Odd lot of folk these people are!		Drôles de gens que ces gens là.

MORALES

We stand round in the Guardroom doorway,	A la porte du corps de garde
Hoping time will fly,	Pour tuer le temps,
Smoking, gossiping, while observing	On fume, on jase, l'on regarde
Passers-by pass by.	Passer les passants.

CHORUS

All around here,	Sur la place,
(etc.)	*(etc.)*

Micaela, in a blue skirt, with plaits to her shoulders, appears. Shy and embarrassed, she watches the soldiers, comes forward, moves away again, etc..

MORALES
(to the soldiers)

Well here is someone rather sweeter	Regardez donc cette petite
Who seems to have something to say,	Qui semble vouloir nous parler ...
She has! You see, she's turning, we should meet her ...	Voyez, voyez! elle tourne, elle hésite ...

CHORUS

We ought to help, and right away!	A son secours il faut aller!

MORALES
(to Micaela, gallantly)

Well, who d'you want, my charmer?	Que cherchez-vous, la belle?

MICAELA
(simply)

Me? A Corporal of Dragoons.	Moi, je cherche un brigadier.

MORALES
(emphatically)

Here you are,	Je suis là,
That's me!	Voilà!

MICAELA

The Corporal I have come to see is called	Mon brigadier, à moi, s'appelle
Don José ... Do you know him too?	Don José ... le connaissez-vous?

59

MORALES

Don José? Oh yes, indeed we do. | Don José! nous le connaissons tous.

MICAELA
(eagerly)

You do! Then tell me is he now with you here? | Vraiment! Est-il avec vous, je vous prie?

MORALES
(elegantly)

He never was a Corporal in our Platoon, dear. | Il n'est pas brigadier dans notre compagnie.

MICAELA
(disappointed)

And so, he's not in there. | Alors, il n'est pas là?

MORALES

No, dearest charmer, he's not in there,
But very soon he will be here.
He will be here the moment that the new [5]
guard
Relieves the guard that's due to go off duty.

Non, ma charmante, il n'est pas là;
Mais tout à l'heure il y sera.
Il y sera quand la garde montante
Remplacera la garde descendante.

ALL

He will be here the moment that the new
guard
Relieves the guard that's due to go off duty.

Il y sera quand la garde montante
Remplacera la garde descendante.

MORALES
(very gallant)

While you wait for his arrival,
Would you care, my lovely child,
Would you care to take the trouble,
To step inside here awhile?

Mais en attendant qu'il vienne,
Voulez-vous, la belle enfant,
Voulez-vous prendre la peine
D'entrer chez nous un instant?

MICAELA

With you? | Chez vous?

SOLDIERS

Oh do! | Chez nous.

MICAELA
(wittily)

Oh no! No, no,
Many thanks, kind sirs, even so!

Non pas, non pas,
Grand merci, messieurs les soldats.

MORALES

Step inside, dear, don't be frightened,
For I promise while you're there,
We will show, towards your person,
The great respect you inspire.

Entrez sans crainte, mignonne,
Je vous promets qu'on aura,
Pour votre chère personne,
Tous les égards qu'il faudra.

MICAELA

I am sure you will, all the same,
I shall return, that will be best, I'll try
again!

Je n'en doute pas, cependant,
Je reviendrai, je reviendrai, c'est
plus prudent.

(She laughs as she repeats Morales's phrase.)

I shall return the moment that the new
guard
Relieves the guard that's due to go off duty.

Je reviendrai quand la garde montante
Remplacera la garde descendante.

SOLDIERS

Stay here until the moment that the
new guard
Relieves the guard that's due to go off duty.

Il faut rester car la garde montante
Va remplacer la garde descendante.

60

	(surrounding Micaela)
Oh, you must stay!	Vous resterez.

MICAELA
(trying to get away)

No, no, I can't!	Non pas! non pas!

SOLDIERS

Oh, you must stay!	Vous resterez.

MICAELA

No, no, I can't!	Non pas! non pas!
No! No! So goodbye,	Non! Non! Au revoir,
My friends, I must go!	Messieurs les soldats.

She escapes and runs off.

MORALES

The bird has flown,	L'oiseau s'envole,
We're left alone!	On s'en console.
Once again we'll have to try	Reprenons notre passe-temps
Observing passers-by pass by!	Et regardons passer les gens.

CHORUS

All around here	[4]	Sur la place
(etc.)		(etc.)

For the 'Scène et Pantomime' inserted here, see page 125.

Bugles and fifes can be heard very faintly in the distance, playing a military march. The new guard is arriving. The officer comes out of the Guardroom. A bugle call on stage. The soldiers go to take their lances and line up in front of the Guardroom. The passers-by form a group on the right to watch the changing of the guard. The sound of the military march comes nearer and nearer . . . The new guard finally enters from the left and crosses the bridge. First two fifes and a bugle. Then a troop of little urchins taking very long steps to keep pace with the Dragoons — the children should be as small as possible. Lieutenant Zuniga and Corporal Don José behind the children, then the Dragoons with their lances.

Scene Two. *The same, Don José, the Lieutenant / No. 2 March and Chorus of Urchins.* [6]

CHORUS OF URCHINS

With the guard that comes on duty	Avec la garde montante,
We are marching, here we are!	Nous arrivons, nous voilà!
Sound trumpet, sound very loudly!	Sonne, trompette éclatante!
Ta ra ta ta, ta ra ta ta.	Ta ra ta ta, ta ra ta ta.
We are proper little soldiers,	Nous marchons la tête haute
Heads well up we march along,	Comme de petits soldats,
We keep in step with the music,	Marquant, sans faire de faute,
Left! Right! We're never wrong. *(shouted)*	Une, deux, marquant le pas.
Shoulders well back when we're marching,	Les épaules en arrière
Chest well out, we're on parade,	Et la poitrine en dehors,
Arms held, like this, from the shoulder,	Les bras de cette manière,
With the fingers down the side.	Tombant tout le long du corps.
With the guard that comes on duty	Avec la garde montante,
We are marching. Here we are!	Nous arrivons, nous voilà.
Sound trumpet, sound very loudly!	Sonne, trompette éclatante!
Ta ra ta ta, ta ra ta ta.	Ta ra ta ta, ta ra ta ta.

ZUNIGA
(over the last bars of the Chorus)

Guard, Halt! Left turn! Stand at ease!	Halte! Repos!

The new guard lines up on the right, facing the old guard. As soon as the urchins, who have stopped on the right in front of the curious onlookers, stop singing, the officers salute with their swords and begin to speak in low voices. Sentries are changed.

ZUNIGA
(over the music of the Mélodrame*)

Sentries, attention! Left turn!
To your posts! Quick march!

MORALES
(aside to Don José)

A pretty girl came to ask for you just now. She said that she'd come back.	Il y a une jolie fille qui est venue te demander. Elle a dit qu'elle reviendrait . . .

DON JOSE

A pretty girl?	Une jolie fille?

MORALES

Yes, and nicely dressed, a blue skirt, with plaits to her shoulders . . .	Oui, et gentiment habillée, une jupe bleu, des nattes tombant sur les épaules . . .

DON JOSE

That's Micaela . . . That could only be Micaela!	C'est Micaela. Ce ne peut être que Micaela.

MORALES

She didn't give her name.	Elle n'a pas dit son nom.

LIEUTENANT OF THE OLD GUARD (ANDRES)
(to Morales over the end of the Mélodrame)

Come on, come on! Guard! Attention!
(to the soldiers over the bugle call)
Left turn! Quick march!

Sentries have been changed. Bugles are sounded. The old guard marches out in front of the new guard. The urchins, behind the bugle and fifes of the old guard, exactly in the same positions as they were with the new guard.

CHORUS OF URCHINS

With the guard that goes off duty	Et la garde descendante
Off to barracks here we are.	Rentre chez elle et s'en va.
Sound trumpet, sound very loudly!	Sonne, trompette éclatante!
Ta ra ta ta, ta ra ta ta.	Ta ra ta ta, ta ra ta ta.
We are proper little soldiers,	Nous marchons le tête haute
Heads well up we march along,	Comme de petits soldats,
We keep in step with the music,	Marquant, sans faire de faute,
Left! Right! We're never wrong. *(shouted)*	Une, deux, marquant le pas.
Shoulders well back when we're † marching,	Les épaules en arrière
Chest well out, we're on parade!	Et la poitrine en dehors,
Arms held like this from the shoulder,	Les bras de cette manière
With the fingers down the side.	Tombant tout le long du corps.
With the guard that goes off duty	Et la garde descendante
Off to barracks here we are.	Rentre chez elle et s'en va.
Sound trumpet, sound very loudly,	Sonne, trompette éclatante,
Ta ra ta ta, ta ra ta ta.	Ta ra ta ta, ta ra ta ta.

Soldiers, urchins and onlookers go out upstage; the chorus, fifes and bugles grow gradually fainter. Meantime, Zuniga, in charge of the new guard silently inspects his men. Once the chorus of urchins and the fifes can no longer be heard, Zuniga says: "Present lances! Slope lances! Guard, fall out!" The Dragoons place their lances in the rack, then go into the Guardroom. Don José and Zuniga remain on stage.

---

* Because the page of *Mélodrame* music times beautifully with the José/Morales dialogue and the Changing of the Sentries business, it does not add to the length of the opera and helps to remind us of the atmosphere of José's and Micaela's childhood.

† The second verse is often cut following the 1875 vocal score.

Scene Three. *Zuniga, Don José.*

ZUNIGA

Tell me, corporal . . .	Dites-moi, brigadier?

JOSE
(rising)

Yes, Señor.	Mon lieutenant.

ZUNIGA

I've only been with this regiment two days [and I've never been to Sevilla before.] What's that [big] building?	Je ne suis dans le régiment que depuis deux jours et jamais je n'étais venu à Séville. Qu'est-ce que c'est que ce grand bâtiment?

JOSE

The tobacco factory . . .	C'est la manufacture de tabacs . . .

ZUNIGA

And do women work there? . . .	Ce sont des femmes qui travaillent là? . . .

JOSE

Yes, Señor. [They are not there at the moment; they'll soon be back from their dinner. And I can promise you that there will be quite a crowd here then to watch them go in	Oui, mon lieutenant. Elles n'y sont pas maintenant; tout à l'heure, après leur dîner, elles vont revenir. Et je vous réponds qu'alors il y aura du monde pour les voir passer.

ZUNIGA

Are there a lot of them?	Elles sont beaucoup?

JOSE

My word, yes! — at least four or five hundred who roll cigars in a huge room.]	Ma foi, elles sont bien quatre ou cinq cents qui roulent des cigares dans une grande salle . . .

ZUNIGA

That ought to be interesting!	Ce doit être curieux.

JOSE

Yes, but men aren't allowed in without a pass.	Oui, mais les hommes ne peuvent pas entrer dans cette salle sans une permission . . .

ZUNIGA

Why's that?	Ah!

JOSE

Because when it's hot the younger girls don't wear much.	Parce que, lorsqu'il fait chaud, ces ouvrières se mettent à leur aise, surtout les jeunes.

ZUNIGA

Then there *are* young ones?	Il y en a de jeunes?

JOSE

Oh yes Señor.	Mais oui, mon lieutenant.

ZUNIGA

Are they pretty?	Et de jolies?

ZUNIGA
(laughing)

[I suppose so . . . But] to be honest, [although I've been on guard here several times already] I'm not sure, because I've never really looked at them . . .	Je le suppose . . . Mais à vous dire vrai, et bien que j'aie été de garde ici plusieurs fois déjà, je n'en suis pas bien sûr, car je ne les ai jamais beaucoup regardées . . .

ZUNIGA

[Oh, come on!

Allons donc!...

JOSE

What do you expect?]... These Andalusian girls frighten me. I don't understand them; [they are always getting at you... never a word of sense...]

Que voulez-vous?... ces Andalouses me font peur. Je ne suis pas fait à leurs manières, toujours à railler... jamais un mot de raison...

ZUNIGA

Besides we've a weakness for blue skirts and plaits to the shoulders?

Et puis nous avons un faible pour les jupes bleues, et pour les nattes tombant sur les épaules...

JOSE
(*laughing*)

[Ah, Señor heard what Morales was saying?

Ah! mon lieutenant a entendu ce que disait Moralès?

ZUNIGA

Yes...]

Oui...

JOSE

I won't deny it... the blue skirt, and plaits, is the Basque dress... it reminds me of home...

Je ne le nierai pas... la jupe bleue, les nattes, c'est le costume de Navarre... ça me rappelle le pays...

ZUNIGA

So you're Basque?

Vous êtes Navarrais?

JOSE

Yes, from a very old Christian family.* [Don José Lizzarabengoa is my name.] I was intended for the Church [and they put me to study, but I made little progress.] My passion for playing Pelota was too great. One day, a boy [from Alava whom] I'd just beaten, picked a quarrel with me. This time I beat him so hard that I had to leave the country. I joined the army here. [My father was already dead.] My mother came and settled outside Sevilla... with little Micaela... an orphan whom she'd adopted [and who would not leave her].

Et vieux chrétien.* Don José Lizzarabengoa, c'est mon nom... On voulait que je fusse d'église, et l'on m'a fait étudier. Mais je ne profitais guère, j'aimais trop jouer à la paume... Un jour que j'avais gagné, un gars de l'Alava me cherche querelle; j'eus encore l'avantage, mais cela m'obligea de quitter le pays. Je me fis soldat! Je n'avais plus mon père; ma mère me suivit et vint s'établir à dix lieues de Séville... avec la petite Micaela... c'est une orpheline que ma mère a recueillie, et qui n'a pas voulu se séparer d'elle...

ZUNIGA

And how old is 'little Micaela'?

Et quel âge a-t-elle, la petite Micaela?

JOSE

Seventeen...

Dix-sept ans...

ZUNIGA

Why didn't you say so before?... Now I see why you couldn't tell me if the factory girls were pretty or plain.

Il fallait dire cela tout de suite... Je comprends maintenant pourquoi vous ne pouvez pas me dire si les ouvrières de la manufacture sont jolies ou laides.

(*The factory bell rings.*)

---

* Rather as we would say, 'We came over with the Conqueror'. The 'new' Christians were the converts from Islam with at least part Moorish blood. According to Mérimée, José had his family tree on parchment at home.

(*over Introduction to No. 3 Chorus and Scene*)

There goes the factory bell, Señor. Now you can judge for yourself... [I'm going to make a chain for the priming pin for my rifle.]	Voici la cloche qui sonne, mon lieutenant, et vous allez pouvoir juger par vous-même... Quant à moi je vais faire une chaîne pour attacher mon épinglette.

Scene Four. *The square begins to fill with young men who come and stand where the girls will pass. The soldiers come out of the Guard house. Don José sits making his chain, quite oblivious of what is happening. Don José, Soldiers, Young Men and Cigarette Girls. / No.* 3 *Chorus and Scene* †

YOUNG MEN

There's the factory bell, so we take our places,	La cloche a sonné, nous, des ouvrières,
Lying here in wait till the girls arrive;	Nous venons ici guetter le retour;
Then we follow you, dusky little beauties,	Et nous vous suivrons, brunes cigarières,
Murmuring in your ear tender words of love!	En vous murmurant des propos d'amour!

(*The cigarette girls appear, cigarettes between their lips. They come under the bridge and slowly onto the stage.*)

SOLDIERS

There they are! With gaze unashamed, Looks so provoking!	Voyez-les... Regards impudents, Mine coquette!
Cigarettes between their red lips, Lazily smoking!	Fumant toutes, du bout des dents La cigarette.

CIGARETTE GIRLS

Our eyes slowly follow where Smoke is curling, Slowly curling, Scenting the air As it rises ever higher. And the smoke that we inhale Gently rises, Gently rises, Into the head like a charm To all the senses. Those loving words lovers repeat In your ear, Are but smoke! Their passion and all the vows That they swear, Are but smoke! Our eyes slowly follow where Smoke is curling, Ever higher. It curls as it floats To the sky, Ever higher!	[7] Dans l'air nous suivons des yeux La fumée, La fumée Qui vers les cieux Monte, monte parfumée. Cela monte gentiment A la tête, A la tête, Tout doucement, cela vous met L'âme en fête! Le doux parler, le doux parler Des amants, C'est fumée! Leurs transports, leurs transports Et leurs sermonts, C'est fumée! Dans l'air nous suivons des yeux La fumée! La fumée Qui monte, en tournant Vers les cieux! La fumée!

YOUNG MEN*
(*to the Cigarette Girls*)

You should not be so heartless, Cruel beauties do hear us. You whom we love and prize, Whom we all idolize!	Sans faire les cruelles, Écoutez-nous les belles, Vous que nous adorons, Que nous idolâtrons.

---

† Bizet altered this very considerably from the libretto, cutting two refrains, and expanding some other lines in order to avoid the conventional forms.

* This interjection for the tenors and the reprise are often cut in performance, following the 1875 vocal score.

Those loving words in your ear | Le doux parler des amants,
And their passion and their vows here | Leurs transports et leurs serments
All will vanish | C'est fumée,
As the smoke does. | C'est fumée.
Our eyes slowly follow the smoke | Dans l'air nous suivons la fumée
As it curls, as it floats | Qui monte, en tournant
To the sky, | Vers les cieux!
Ever higher! | La fumée!

Scene Five. *The same, Carmen.*

SOLDIERS

But we have not yet seen our Carmencita. | Nous ne voyons pas la Carmencita.

CIGARETTE GIRLS AND YOUNG MEN

Here she comes! | La voilà!
She is here! | La voilà!
Here is our Carmencita! | Voilà la Carmencita!

Enter Carmen. Her costume and manner of entering are exactly as Mérimée described. She wears a bunch of acacia flowers in her corsage and holds a single bloom at the corner of her mouth. Three or four young men enter with her. They follow her, surround her and talk to her. She flirts and chatters with them. Don José looks up. He looks at Carmen, then returns to working quietly on his chain.

YOUNG MEN
(*surrounding Carmen*)

Carmen! Like your shadow we follow you! | Carmen! sur tes pas nous nous pressons tous!
Carmen! Oh be kind and answer us do! | Carmen! sois gentille au moins réponds-nous!

And tell us which day to hope for your love! | Et dis-nous quel jour tu nous aimeras!

CARMEN
(*gaily, having quickly thrown a glance at Don José*)
[3b]

When will *you* have my love? Good Lord! How can I tell . . . | Quand je vous aimerai? ma foi, je ne sais pas . . .
Perhaps not at all, tomorrow maybe! | Peut-être jamais! . . . peut-être demain!
| (*firmly*)
It won't be today . . . you will see. | Mais pas aujourd'hui, c'est certain.

No. 4 Habanera

Love's a bird that will live in freedom, [8] | L'amour est un oiseau rebelle
That no man ever learned to tame, | Que nul ne peut apprivoiser,
And in vain men may call and call her | Et c'est bien en vain qu'on l'appelle,
If she's no mind to play their game! | S'il lui convient de refuser.
They'll find nothing they do will tempt her, | Rien n'y fait, menace ou prière,
The one tries charm, the other's dumb! | L'un parle bien, l'autre se tait;

And that other's the one I fancy, | Et c'est l'autre que je préfère,
He may not talk, but he's the one! | Il n'a rien dit, mais il me plaît.

Oh love was born to gipsy life, [9] | L'amour est enfant de Bohême,
A life that's free, that is as free as air; | Il n'a jamais, jamais connu de loi,
You may not love me, yet I love you, | Si tu ne m'aimes pas, je t'aime;
But if I love you, then you take care! | Mais si je t'aime, prends garde à toi!

But this bird that you thought you'd taken | L'oiseau que tu croyais surprendre
Has flapped her wings and flown away; | Battit de l'aile et s'envola;
When love's gone then you sit there waiting, | L'amour est loin, tu peux l'attendre;

You give up waiting, down she'll fly!
All around you she'll fly so quickly,
She's there, she's gone, she's back in view,
Think you've caught her and she'll escape
you,
Think you've escaped and she's caught
you!

Oh love was born to gipsy life,
A life that's free, that is as free as air,
You may not love me, yet I love you;
But if I love you, then you take care!

Tu ne l'attends plus . . . il est là!
Tout autour de toi, vite, vite,
Il vient, s'en va, puis il revient;
Tu crois le tenir, il t'évite;
Tu crois l'éviter, il te tient.

L'amour est enfant de Bohême,
Il n'a jamais, jamais connu de loi;
Si tu ne m'aimes pas, je t'aime;
Mais si je t'aime, prends garde à toi!

No. 5 Scene

YOUNG MEN

Carmen! Like your shadow we follow
you!
Carmen! Oh be kind and answer us do!

Carmen! sur tes pas nous nous pressons
tous!
Carmen! sois gentille au moins réponds-
nous!

The young men surround Carmen. She looks at them and then at Don José . . . She hesitates . . . she seems to be going into the factory . . . then she retraces her steps and goes straight up to Don José, who is still busying himself with the chain for his priming pin.

[3b]

CARMEN

Eh! Friend, what are you making?

† Eh! compère, qu'est-ce que tu fais
là? . . .

JOSE
(looks up and sees Carmen in front of him)

A brass wire chain for my priming pin.

Je fais une chaîne avec du fil de laiton,
une chaîne pour attacher mon épinglette.

CARMEN
(laughing)

Your pin, really! Your pin . . . Ah, pin up
of my soul! . . .

Ton épinglette, vraiment! ton épinglette . . . épinglier de mon âme! . . .

She takes an acacia flower from her corsage and throws it at Don José. He rises sharply. The flower has fallen at his feet. General laughter; the factory bell sounds once again. Exeunt factory girls and young men, singing:)

Oh love! Oh love was born to gipsy
life,
(*etc.*)

L'amour est enfant de Bohême,

(*etc.*)

Scene Four. *Carmen runs into the factory. The young men leave to the right and the left. The lieutenant, who had been chatting with some factory girls during the scene, leaves them and follows the soldiers into the Guardhouse. Don José stands looking at the flower, which has fallen in front of him.*

JOSE

[And what's that supposed to mean? . . .]
What impudence! . . .

Qu'est-ce que cela veut dire, ces façons-
là? . . . Quelle effronterie! . . .

(smiling)

And all because I wouldn't pay her any

Tout ça parce que je ne faisais pas

---

† There is an alternative dialogue for this, which may be translated as:
CARMEN: Eh! Friend, will you give me that chain for my keys?
JOSE: It's for the priming pin of my rifle.
CARMEN: Ah, señor needs pins! . . . He makes lace! . . . (*laughter*) Make me seven yards for a
        mantilla, lacemaker to my soul!

And all because I wouldn't pay her any attention . . . [So, like women and cats who never come when you call them — but always come when you don't, she came . . .]

attention à elle! . . . Alors, suivant l'usage des femmes et des chats qui ne viennent pas quand on les appelle et qui viennent quand on ne les appelle pas, elle est venue . . .

(*He looks at the flower at his feet and picks it up.*)

The way she threw this flower! . . . [Right between my eyes! . . .] like a bullet!

Avec quelle adresse elle me l'a lancée, cette fleur . . . là, juste entre les deux yeux . . . ça m'a fait l'effet d'une balle qui m'arrivait . . .

(*He smells the flower.*)

What a scent it has! . . . If there *are* witches, she's one for certain!

Comme c'est fort! . . . Certainement, s'il y a des sorcières, cette fille-là en est une.

Scene Seven. *Don José, Micaela*

MICAELA

Señor Corporal?

Monsieur le brigadier?

JOSE
(*hurriedly hiding the acacia flower*)

What? . . . What's that?

Quoi? . . . Qu'est-ce que c'est? . . .

(*seeing her*)

Micaela! . . . it's you . . .

Micaela! . . . c'est toi . . .

MICAELA

It's me! . . .

C'est moi! . . .

JOSE

[And you've come from home? . . .

Et tu viens de là-bas? . . .

MICAELA

And I've come from home . . .] your mother sent me . . .

Et je viens de là-bas . . . C'est votre mère qui m'envoie . . .

JOSE

[My mother . . .]

Ma mère . . .

No. 6 Duet

JOSE
(*moved*)

Oh tell me all about her! How she was when you left her?

Parle-moi de ma mère! Parle-moi de ma mère!

MICAELA
(*simply*)

I've come instead of her, with something that she gave me;
Here's a letter.

[10] J'apporte de sa part, fidèle messagère,
Cette lettre.

JOSE
(*delighted*)

From my mother!

Une lettre.

MICAELA

And here's some money too . . .

Et puis un peu d'argent.

(*She gives him a small purse.*)

To help you out a little with your pay . . .
And then . . .

Pour ajoutter à votre traitement,
Et puis . . .

JOSE

And then?

Et puis?

MICAELA
(*hesitating*)

And then . . . Oh, no, I dare not,

Et puis . . . vraiment je n'ose!

68

And then ... there's something else I bring you
Worth more than all your pay, and which for any son
Will have a value all its own.

Et puis ... encore une autre chose
Qui vaut mieux que l'argent et qui, pour un bon fils,
Aura sans doute plus de prix.

JOSE

This other something, you must tell me What it is ...

Cette autre chose, quelle est-elle? Parle donc ...

MICAELA

Yes, I'll tell you now.
What I received from her I now will give to you.
As we both were returning home from Church this morning,
Taking my arm gently in hers: —
"Now go", your mother said, "to the town, Micaela,
It isn't very far there, and when you reach Sevilla
You look for my dear son, my José, my own boy!
Say his mother never forgets him,　[11]
Has him night and day in her mind ...
Though he did wrong, yet she forgives him,
And that she hopes that he'll return.
All I've said now be sure you tell him,
Just as though I were there to see;
And then the kiss that I give you now,
With my love give to him from me".

Oui, je parlerai.
Ce que l'on m'a donné, je vous le donnerai.
Votre mère avec moi sortait de la chapelle,

Et c'est alors qu'en m'embrassant:
Tu vas, m'a-t-elle dit, t'en aller à la ville:
La route n'est pas longue, une fois à Séville

Tu chercheras mon fils, mon José, mon enfant!
Et tu lui diras que sa mère
Songe nuit et jour à l'absent ...
Qu'elle regrette et qu'elle espère,

Qu'elle pardonne et qu'elle attend.
Tout cela, n'est-ce-pas, mignonne,
De ma part tu le lui diras;
Et ce baiser que je te donne
De ma part tu le lui rendras.

JOSE
(*very moved*)

Then it's true she forgives me!

Un baiser de ma mère?

MICAELA

And she sends you a kiss.
José, I give it you as she then gave it me.

Un baiser pour son fils!
José, je vous le rends, comme je l'ai promis.

Micaela stands on tiptoe and gives José an unselfconsciously maternal kiss. Don José, very moved, lets her kiss him.

JOSE
(*very moved*)

She's there before my eyes! ... And there's [12] the village I remember!
Oh happy days now gone by! Oh land that I held so dear!
You fill my heart with strength and give me courage.
Oh memory so dear,
My mother standing there, that village I remember.
She's there before my eyes ...
(*etc.*)

Ma mère, je la vois! ... oui je revois mon village!
O souvenirs d'autrefois, doux souvenirs du pays!
Vous remplissez mon cœur de force et de courage.
O souvenirs chéris,
Ma mère je la vois, je revois mon village.
Ma mère, je la revois ...
(*etc.*)

MICAELA

She's there before his eyes ...
(*etc.*)

Sa mère il la revoit ...
(*etc.*)

JOSE
(*to himself, looking towards the factory*)

Who knows of what demon I should have been the prey!

Qui sait de quel démon j'allais être la proie!

(*pulling himself together*)

Even from far my Mother breaks the charm

Même de loin, ma mère me défend,

69

(impulsively)

And by the kiss that she has sent me She drives the danger off and keeps her son from harm!	Et ce baiser qu'elle m'envoie Ecarte le péril et sauve son enfant!

MICAELA
(straightforwardly)

But what demon and what harm? I do not understand . . . Tell me what do you mean?	Quel démon, quel péril? je ne comprends pas bien . . . Que veut dire cela?

JOSE

Nothing! Nothing! Let's talk of you, dear Micaela; So will you be back there today?	Rien! Rien! Parlons de toi, la messagère; Tu vas retourner au pays?

MICAELA

Yes, by this evening . . . I'll see your mother in the morning.	Oui, ce soir même, . . . demain je verrai votre mère.

JOSE
(eagerly)

Well when you do, remember . . . Tell her from me How much I love her and revere her, How true my repentance today. I'd like her, though we are parted, To be proud of her boy! All I've said now be sure you tell her, Just as though she were here to see! And then the kiss that I give you now, With my love give to her from me!	Tu la verras! Eh bien! tu lui diras: Que son fils l'aime et la venère Et qu'il se repent aujourd'hui; Il veut que la-bàs sa mère Soit contente de lui! Tout cela, n'est-ce pas, mignonne, De ma part, tu le lui diras! Et ce baiser que je te donne De ma part tu le lui rendras!

[11]
(He kisses her.)

MICAELA
(simply)

I promise that I will . . . and with love from her son, José, I'll give it her as you would like it done.	Oui, je vous le promets . . . de la part de son fils José, je le rendrai comme je l'ai promis.

Reprise of Duet. [12]

JOSE

Wait a moment . . . I'll read her letter . . .	Attends un peu maintenant . . . je vais lire sa lettre . . .

MICAELA

[I'll wait, Don José, I'll wait.]	J'attendrai, monsieur le brigadier, j'attendrai.

JOSE
(He kisses the letter before he begins to read.)

"Keep up your good conduct, my boy! They've promised to make you a Quartermaster. Then perhaps you can leave the service and [make them give you a little house. I'm getting very old. You could] come back near me and get married. We shouldn't have great difficulty in finding you a wife, [and I know very well whom I should advise you to choose: —] the one who brings you my letter . . . There is no-one more understanding or sweeter . . . "	Ah! "continue à te bien conduire, mon enfant! L'on t'a promis de te faire maréchal des logis, peut-être alors pourras-tu quitter le service, te faire donner une petite place et revenir près de moi. Je commence à me faire bien vieille. Tu reviendrais près de moi et tu te marierais, nous n'aurions pas, je pense, grand'peine à te trouver une femme, et je sais bien, quant à moi, celle que je te conseillerais de choisir: c'est tout justement celle qui te porte ma lettre . . . Il n'y en a pas de plus sage et de plus gentille . . .

I'd better go...   Il vaut mieux que je ne sois pas là!

JOSE

[But why?...]   Pourquoi donc?...

MICAELA

I've just remembered that your mother   Je viens de me rappeler que votre mère
asked me to get a few things... [I'll get   m'a chargée de quelques petits achats; je
them now...]   vais m'en occuper tout de suite.

JOSE

Wait! I've finished...   Attends un peu, j'ai fini...

MICAELA

[You can finish it when I'm not   Vous finirez quand je ne serai plus
there...   là...

JOSE

But the answer?...   Mais la réponse?...

MICAELA

I'll come back and collect it before I   Je reviendrai la prendre avant mon
leave and I'll take it to your   départ et je la porterai à votre mère...
mother... Goodbye!   Adieu!

JOSE

Micaela!   Micaela!

MICAELA

No, no... I'll come back, I'd rather...   Non, non... je reviendrai, j'aime mieux
I'll come back, I'll come back...]*   cela... je reviendrai, je reviendrai...
                        (*She runs out.*)

Scene Eight. *José, Cigarette Girls, Zuniga, Soldiers. / No. 7 Chorus*

JOSE
(*reading*)

"There is no-one sweeter or more   "Il n'y en a pas de plus sage, ni de plus
understanding... and no-one who loves   gentille... il n'y en a pas surtout qui
you as much... [and if you wanted]..."   t'aime davantage... et si tu voulais..."
Yes Mother [I'll do what you want], I'll   Oui, ma mère, oui, je ferai ce que tu
marry Micaela. As for that gipsy with   désires... j'épouserai Micaela, et quant
her witch's flowers...]   à cette bohémienne, avec ses fleurs qui
                                                 ensorcellent...

*Just as he is going to take out the flower from his tunic, there is a great uproar in the
factory. Zuniga enters followed by soldiers.*

ZUNIGA

Now then! Now then! What's going on?   Eh bien! eh bien! qu'est-ce qui arrive?

The Cigarette Girls rush out half-undressed.

CHORUS OF CIGARETTE GIRLS

Come and help! Can't you hear the row?   Au secours! n'entendez-vous pas?
Come and help! Separate them now.   Au secours! messieurs les soldats!

FIRST GROUP OF WOMEN

Carmen's the one to blame!   C'est la Carmencita!

SECOND GROUP OF WOMEN

No, no, it wasn't her fault!   Non, non, ce n'est pas elle!

---

* This dialogue may be alternatively shortened: "I'll come back... I'd rather... I'll
come back".

It was.   C'est elle.

It was not.   Pas du tout.

It was, it was, she hit her!   Si fait, si fait c'est elle!
She hit her first — we're telling you!   Elle a porté les premiers coups!

Don't listen to their lies, Señor, it isn't   Ne les écoutez pas, monsieur, écoutez-
true!   nous,
    It isn't true!   Écoutez-nous,
    It isn't true!   Écoutez-nous!

Manuelita had said   La Manuelita disait,
And she repeated it loudly,   Et répétait à voix haute
She was going to buy a donkey,   Qu'elle achèterait sans faute
Pedigree, and highly bred.   Un âne qui lui plaisait.

Carmencita down the room   Alors la Carmencita
Retorted as usual, rudely,   Railleuse à son ordinaire,
"Why d'you want to ride a donkey?   Dit: un âne, pourquoi faire?
You'd look better on a broom!"   Un balais te suffira.

Manuelita replied,   Manueliota riposta
"If *you* ever need a donkey   Et dit à sa camarade:
For a certain little journey,   Pour certaine promenade,
He'll serve you for such a ride."   Mon âne te servira.

"When they take you to the jail   Et ce jour-là tu pourras
You can ride there like a lady,   A bon droit faire la fière;
Two police behind the donkey,   Deux laquais suivront derrière
Swotting flies upon your tail!"*   T'émouchant à tour de bras.

Thereupon each of the pair,   Là-dessus toutes les deux
Grabbed a great handful of hair,   Se sont prises aux cheveux,
Grabbed the other by the hair!   Se sont prises aux cheveux!

To hell with them and their palaver!   Au diable tout ce bavardage!
(*to Don José*)
You there, José, just take a couple of men,   Prenez, José, deux hommes avec vous,
Go inside and find out who is causing   Et voyez là dedans qui cause ce tapage!
the row there!

*Don José takes two men with him and goes into the factory. Meanwhile the women
struggle and argue.*

Carmen's the one to blame!   C'est la Carmencita.

No, no, it wasn't her fault!   Non, non, ce n'est pas elle.
(*etc.*)   (*etc.*)

---

* Women of ill repute were put on a donkey, facing the tail, and whipped through the
town.

(deafened — to the soldiers)

Hi, you!
Get all of these women here out of my
way!

Holà!
Éloignez-moi toutes ces femme-là!

ALL THE WOMEN

Señor, señor, don't listen to their lies!
It isn't true! It isn't true!

Monsieur! Monsieur! ne les écoutez pas!
Écoutez-nous! Écoutez-nous!

SOLDIERS
(They push the women back and separate them.)

Go on, get over there
And hold your tongue. Go on, get over
there!

Tout doux! Tout doux!
Éloignez-vous et taisez-vous.

WOMEN

It isn't true!

Écoutez-nous!

SOLDIERS

Get over there!

Tout doux.

The Cigarette Girls slip between the soldiers who are trying to push them back. They rush at Zuniga and repeat their story.

FIRST GROUP

Carmen's the one to blame.
(etc.)

C'est la Carmencita
(etc.)

SECOND GROUP

Manuelita's to blame.
(etc.)

C'est la Manuelita
(etc.)

SOLDIERS
(pushing the women back again)

Go on, get over there
And hold your tongue! Go on get over
there!

Tout doux! Tout doux!
Éloignez-vous et taisez-vous.

The soldiers finally succeed in pushing the women back. They are kept at a distance around the square by a line of dragoons. Carmen appears at the factory entrance, led by Don José and two soldiers.

Scene Nine. *The same, Carmen*

ZUNIGA

Well, Corporal . . . now that we have a
little quiet . . . what did you find in
there? . . .

Voyons, brigadier . . . Maintenant que
nous avons un peu de silence . . . qu'est-
ce que vous avez trouvé là dedans? . . .

JOSE

[The first thing I saw was about] three
hundred screaming, half-naked women,
[making such a racket that you couldn't
hear yourself think . . .] One of them, on
the ground*, [her four paws in the air,]
was screaming, "A priest, a priest, I'm
dead!" [On her face was an X which had
just been cut with two strokes of a
knife.] Opposite the wounded woman I
saw . . .

J'ai d'abord trouvé trois cents femmes,
criant, hurlant, gesticulant, faisant un
tapage à ne pas entendre Dieu
tonner . . . D'un côté il y en avait une,
les quatres fers en l'air, qui criait:
Confession! Confession! . . . je suis morte
. . . Elle avait sur la figure un X qu'on
venait de lui marquer en deux coups de
couteau . . . en face de la blessée j'ai
vu . . .

(He stops as Carmen looks at him.)

---

* Alternative: with a cross cut on her face.

ZUNIGA	
Well? ...	Eh bien? ...
JOSE	
I saw the Señorita ...	J'ai vu mademoiselle ...
ZUNIGA	
[Señorita Carmencita?	Mademoiselle Carmencita?
JOSE	
Yes, Señor ...	Oui, mon lieutenant ...
ZUNIGA	
And what did Señorita Carmencita say?	Et qu'est-ce qu'elle disait, mademoiselle Carmencita?
JOSE	
She didn't say anything, Señor, she gritted her teeth and rolled her eyes like a chameleon.	Elle ne disait rien, mon lieutenant, elle serrait les dents et rouler des yeux comme un caméléon.

CARMEN

I was provoked ...] I was only defending myself ... [The Señor Corporal will confirm that ...	On m'avait provoquée ... je n'ai fait que me défendre ... Monsieur le brigadier vous le dira ...
	(to José)
Won't you, Señor Corporal?]	N'est-ce pas, monsieur le brigadier?

JOSE
(after a moment's hesitation)

[In the uproar, all I could gather was that] apparently these two were arguing and [at the end of the argument] the Señorita with her trimming knife [she used for cigars] drew an X on her friend's face ...	Tout ce que j'ai pu comprendre au milieu du bruit, c'est qu'une discussion s'etait élevée entre ces deux dames, et qu'à la suite de cette discussion, mademoiselle, avec le couteau dont elle coupait le bout des cigars, avait commencé à dessiner des croix de saint André sur le visage de sa camarade ...

(Zuniga looks at Carmen. After a glance at Don José and a shrug of her shoulders, she is once more impassive.)

[The situation seemed clear to me. I asked the Señorita to follow me ... She started to resist ... thought better of it ... Then followed me like a lamb!]	Le cas m'a paru clair. J'ai prié mademoiselle de me suivre ... Elle a d'abord fait un mouvement comme pour résister ... puis elle s'est résignée ... et m'a suivi, douce comme un mouton!

ZUNIGA

[And what about the other woman's wound?	Et la blessure de l'autre femme?

JOSE

It's very slight, Señor, just two superficial scratches.]	Très légère, mon lieutenant, deux balafres à fleur de peau.

ZUNIGA
(to Carmen)

Well, my beautiful, you've heard the Corporal? ...	Eh bien! la belle, vous avez entendu le brigadier? ...
	(to José)
I take it that's the truth?	Je n'ai pas besoin de vous demander si vous avez dit la vérité.

JOSE

On the word of a Basque, Señor.	Foi de Navarrais, mon lieutenant!

Carmen turns sharply round, looking at Don José again.

Well, . . . have you anything to say? . . .   Eh bien! . . . vous avez entendu? . . .
Come on, I'm waiting.   Avez-vous quelquechose à répondre? . . .
    parlez, j'attends . . .

Instead of answering, Carmen begins to hum "Tra la la la la". / No. 8 Song and Mélodrame.

CARMEN

Tra, la, la, la, la, la, la, la!   [13] Tra, la, la, la, la, la, la, la!
Though you beat me or burn me, I've   Coupe-moi, brûle-moi, je ne dirai rien;
  nothing to say,
Tra, la, la, la, la, la, la, la!   Tra, la, la, la, la, la, la, la!
For I'll brave all your fire and your steel   Je brave tout, le feu, le fer et le ciel
  — even heaven!   même.

ZUNIGA

It isn't songs that I'm asking for, but an   Ce ne sont pas des chansons que je te
answer.   demande, c'est une réponse.

CARMEN
(*looking impudently at Zuniga*)

Tra, la, la, la, la, la, la, la!   Tra, la, la, la, la, la, la, la,
I've a secret to keep and I'll keep it my   Mon secret je le garde et je le garde
  way!   bien;
Tra, la, la, la, la, la, la, la!   Tra, la, la, la, la, la, la, la!
There's another I love, though you kill   J'en aime un autre et meurs en disant
  me I'll love him.   que je l'aime.

ZUNIGA

Aha! so that's the line we're taking!   Ah! Ah! nous le prenons sur ce ton-là . . .
(*to José*)
One thing's quite clear, isn't it, that   Ce qui est sûr, n'est-ce-pas, c'est qu'il y
there has been a knifing, and that she   a eu des coups de couteau, et que c'est
was the one who used the knife!   elle qui les a donnés . . .

At this moment five or six women from the right succeed in breaking through the line of soldiers and rush to the centre of the stage, shouting "Yes, yes! It was her!" Carmen goes to attack the woman closest to her; Don José prevents her. The soldiers drive off all the women and this time right off the stage. Some soldiers remain in sight, guarding access to the square.

Hey! Hey! You're certainly free with   Eh! Eh! vous avez la main leste
your hands.   décidément.
(*to the soldiers*)
You! Find me some rope!   Trouvez-moi une corde.

A moment of silence. Carmen hums in the most impertinent manner as she watches Zuniga.

SOLDIER
(*bringing a piece of rope*)

The rope, Señor.   Voilà, mon lieutenant.

ZUNIGA
(*to Don José*)

Go and bind those two pretty hands.   Prenez et attachez-moi ces deux jolies
    mains.

(*Carmen, without the least resistance, smiles as she holds out her hands to Don José.*)
It really is a pity, because she's   C'est dommage vraiment, car elle est
attractive! But attractive though you   gentille . . . Mais si gentille que vous
may be, you will go to prison all the   soyez, vous n'en irez pas moins faire un
same. You can sing your gipsy songs   tour à la prison. Vous pourrez y chanter
there, [and the jailer will tell you what   vos chansons de Bohémienne. Le porte-
he thinks of them.]   clefs vous dira ce qu'il en pense.

Carmen's hands are tied. She is made to sit on a bench in front of the Guardroom. She sits quite still, looking down.

I will go and write out the order.	Je vais écrire l'ordre.
	(to Don José)
And *you* can take her.	C'est vous qui la conduirez . . .

He goes out.

Scene Ten. *Carmen, Don José.*

A moment's silence. Carmen raises her eyes and looks at Don José. He turns his back and walks off a few steps. Then he comes back towards Carmen who watches him all the time. [3b]

CARMEN

Where are you taking me?	Où me conduirez-vous?

JOSE

To prison, my poor child . . .	A la prison, ma pauvre enfant . . .

CARMEN

[Eh! what *will* become of me?] Señor officer, have pity on me . . . you are so kind . . .	Hélas! que deviendrai-je? Seigneur officier, ayez pitié de moi . . . Vous êtes si gentil . . .

José does not reply. He turns his back and walks off a few steps and then returns, always under Carmen's gaze.

This rope . . . [the way you've tied it . . .] it's bruising my wrists.	Cette corde, comme vous l'avez serrée, cette corde . . . J'ai les poignets brisés.

JOSE
(approaching Carmen)

If it's hurting you, I can loosen it . . . [The lieutenant told me to bind your hands . . . he didn't tell me . . .]	Si elle vous blesse, je puis le desserrer . . . Le lieutenant m'a dit de vous attacher les mains . . . il ne m'a pas dit . . .

(He unties the rope.)

CARMEN
(softly)

Let me escape and I'll give you a piece of the Bar Lachi, a stone which will make all the girls love you.	Laisse-moi m'échapper, je te donnerai un morceau de la 'bar lachi', une petite pierre qui te fera aimer de toutes les femmes.

JOSE
(moving away)

We aren't here to talk nonsense . . . You're going to prison. That's the order and there's nothing you can do about it.	Nous ne sommes pas ici pour dire des balivernes . . . Il faut aller à la prison. C'est la consigne, et il n'y a pas de remède.

(Silence.)

CARMEN

[Just now] Didn't I hear you say: "On the word of a Basque" — do you come from the North?	Tout à l'heure vous avez dit: foi de Navarrais . . . vous êtes des Provinces? . . .

JOSE

Yes. [I come from Elizondo.	Je suis d'Elizondo . . .

CARMEN

And I from Etchalar . . .	Et moi d'Etchalar . . .

JOSE
(stopping)

From Etchalar! Why that's only four hours from Elizondo.]	D'Etchalar! . . . c'est à quatre heures d'Elizondo, Etchalar.

76

That's where I was born . . . I was carried off by gipsies to Sevilla. I work in the factory to earn my fare back to Navarre, to my poor mother, who has no-one but me to keep her . . . They insult me because I don't belong to this country of pedlars of mouldy oranges, [and those little tramps turned on me simply because I said that all their lads from Sevilla with their knives wouldn't frighten one of our boys with his blue beret and his maquila.] Friend, won't you help a girl from your own country?

Oui, c'est là que je suis née . . . J'ai été emmenée par les Bohémiennes à Séville. Je travaillais à la manufacture pour gagner de quoi retourner en Navarre, prè de ma pauvre mère qui n'a que moi pour soutien . . . On m'a insultée parce que je ne suis pas de ce pays de filous, de marchands d'oranges pourries, et ces coquines se sont mises contre moi parce que je leur ai dit que tous leurs Jacques de Seville avec leurs couteaux ne feraient pas peur à un gars de chez nous avec sons béret bleu et son maquila. Camarade, mon ami, ne ferez-vous rien pour une payse?

JOSE

[You . . . a Basque?]

Vous êtes Navarraise, vous? . . .

CARMEN

Of course!]

Sans doute.

JOSE ·

What nonsense . . . [There's not a word of truth in what you say . . . your eyes alone, your mouth, your complexion . . . all show you're a gipsy . . .

Allons donc . . . il n'y a pas un mot de vrai . . . vos yeux seuls, votre bouche, votre teint . . . Tout vous dit Bohémienne . . .

CARMEN

A gipsy? You believe that?

Bohémienne, tu crois?

JOSE

I'm sure of it . . .]

J'en suis sûr . . .

CARMEN

Alright, but it's very good of me to have taken the trouble to lie to you . . . Yes, I am a gipsy but you'll do what I ask all the same . . . you'll do it because you love me . . .

Au fait, je suis bien bonne de me donner la peine de mentir . . . Oui, je suis Bohémienne, mais tu n'en feras pas moins ce que je te demande . . . Tu le feras parce que tu m'aimes . . .

JOSE

Me! . . .

Moi!

CARMEN

Don't deny it, I know! The way you look at me, the way you speak to me. And the flower that you kept. Oh, you can throw it away now . . . but it won't make any difference. It's stayed long enough near your heart: the spell has worked . . .

Eh! Oui, tu m'aimes . . . ne me dit pas non, je m'y connais! tes regards, la façon dont tu me parles. Et cette fleur que tu as gardée. Oh! tu peux la jeter maintenant . . . cela n'y fera rien. Elle est restée assez de temps sur ton cœur; le charme a opéré . . .

JOSE
(*angrily*)

That's enough, do you hear! I forbid you to speak to me . . .

Ne me parle plus, tu entends, je te défends de parler . . .

CARMEN

Very well, Señor officer. You forbid me to speak, so I'll say nothing . . .

C'est très bien, seigneur officier, c'est très bien. Vous me défendez de parler, je ne parlerai plus . . .

Carmen keeps her eyes fixed on Don José, who walks away; then gradually comes nearer. / No. 9 Song and Duet.

Close by the walls of Sevilla,	[14] Près des remparts de Séville,
Lives my old friend Lillas Pastia,	Chez mon ami Lillas Pastia,
I'll go there to dance Seguidille	J'irai danser la Seguedille
And to drink Manzanilla,	Et boire du Manzanilla,
I will go and visit Lillas Pastia!	J'irai chez mon ami Lillas Pastia!
Yes, but alone it's very boring[1]	Oui, mais toute seule on s'ennuie,
Real pleasures are for two to share...	Et les vrais plaisirs sont à deux...
So to provide amusement for me[2]	Donc, pour me tenir compagnie,
I'll take my latest lover there...	J'emmènerai mon amoureux!...

(laughing)

My latest love!... No, that is over.	Mon amoureux!... il est au diable.
Last night I showed him to the door...	Je l'ai mis à la porte hier...
My wounded heart wants consoling,	Mon pauvre cœur très consolable,
My heart is waiting free as air...	Mon cœur est libre comme l'air...
Tho' I have dozens of admirers	J'ai des galants à la douzaine,
I don't know any who will do;	Mais ils ne sont pas à mon gré;
And here we are, tomorrow's Sunday,	Voici la fin de la semaine:
If I am loved... I will love too.	Qui veut m'aimer? Je l'aimerai!
Who wants my heart... free for the taking...	Qui veut mon âme? Elle est à prendre...
You have arrived at the right time,	Vous arrivez au bon moment!
I'll not stay any longer waiting,	Je n'ai guère le temps d'attendre,
With my new love I'll go along...	Car avec mon nouvel amant...
Close by the walls of Sevilla,	Près des remparts de Séville,
To my old friend Lillas Pastia,	Chez mon ami Lillas Pastia,
I'll go there to dance Seguidille	J'irai danser la Seguedille
And to drink Manzanilla.	Et boire du Manzanilla.
Yes, on Sunday I will visit friend Pastia!	Dimanche, j'irai chez mon ami Pastia!

JOSE

Be quiet, you have been told you must not speak to me.	Tais-toi, je t'avais dit de ne pas me parler.

CARMEN
(innocently)

I didn't speak to you... I sing for my own pleasure,	Je ne te parle pas... je chante pour moi-même,
And I'm thinking... It's surely not forbidden to think.	Et je pense... il n'est pas défendu de penser!
I think of a certain Dragoon,	Je pense à certain officier,
Who loves me, whom in return,	A certain officier qui m'aime,
Yes, in return, I well may learn to love!	Et qu'à mon tour je pourrais bien aimer...

JOSE
(moved)

Carmen!	Carmen!

CARMEN
(pointedly)

But my Dragoon is no swaggering Captain,	Mon officier n'est pas un capitaine:
Nor Lieutenant, oh no, he's only a Corporal;	Pas même un lieutenant, il n'est que brigadier;
But that's good enough for a gipsy girl,	Mais c'est assez pour une Bohémienne,
I've decided to make do with him!	Et je daigne m'en contenter!

JOSE
(untying the rope round Carmen's hands)

Carmen, I am drunk when I hear you,	Carmen, je suis comme un homme ivre
If I weaken, just to be near you,	Si je cède, si je me livre,

---

[1] or: dull for me
[2] or: provide some company

Do you promise you will be true,	Ta promesse, tu la tiendras . . .
And if I love you Carmen, Carmen	Ah! si je t'aime, Carmen, Carmen,
you'll love me too . . .	tu m'aimeras . . .
At Lillas Pastia's, you'll keep	Chez Lillas Pastia, tu le promets?
your word?	
Carmen . . . you'll keep your word . . .	Carmen . . . tu le promets . . .

CARMEN

Yes, there we will dance the	Oui, nous danserons la Seguedille,
Seguidilla,	
And we will drink Manzanilla,	En buvant du Manzanilla,
Close by the walls of Sevilla,	Près des remparts de Séville,
With my old friend Lillas Pastia,	Chez mon ami Lillas Pastia,
There we will dance the Seguidilla	Nous danserons la Seguedille
And we will drink Manzanilla.	Et boirons du Manzanilla.
Tra, la, la, la, la, la, la, la, la, la, la,	Tra, la, la, la, la, la, la, la, la, la, la,

JOSE

The Lieutenant! . . . Take care!	Le lieutenant! . . . Prenez garde!

Don José moves away from Carmen, who goes and sits on her bench again, her hands behind her back. Zuniga returns.

Scene Eleven. *The same, the Lieutenant, then Workers, Soldiers and Townspeople.*
/ No. 10 Finale

ZUNIGA

Here's the order, now go, and mind now	Voici l'ordre, partez et faites bonne
how you guard her!	garde . . .

CARMEN
(aside to José)

On the way I'll give you a shove,	En chemin je te pousserai
With the strength that I know I have	Aussi fort que je le pourrai . . .
So that over you go . . . the rest you leave	Laisse-toi renverser . . . le reste me regarde.
to me.	

(humming and laughing in Zuniga's face)

Oh love that was born to gipsy life, [9]	L'amour est enfant de Bohême,
A life that's free, that is as free as air;	Il n'a jamais, jamais connu de loi;
You may not love me, yet I love you;	Si tu ne m'aimes pas, je t'aime;
If I love you, then you take care!	Si je t'aime, prends garde à toi!

Carmen takes her place between two dragoons, José behind her. Meantime the women and townspeople gradually return kept at a distance by the dragoons. Carmen crosses the stage from left to right, towards the bridge. Arriving at the bridge Carmen pushes José, who lets himself be pushed over. Confusion, chaos. Carmen escapes. When she reaches the centre of the bridge, she stops for a moment and throws the rope over the parapet of the bridge before running off, while the Cigarette Girls surround Zuniga roaring with laughter.

Act Two

Lillas Pastia's inn. Tables on the right and the left. Carmen, Mercedes, Frasquita, Lieutenants Zuniga, Andres and other Officers. They have just finished dinner. The table is in disarray. The officers and the gipsies are smoking cigarettes. Two gipsies are playing guitars in a corner, whilst two gipsy girls are dancing in the middle of the stage. Carmen sits watching the gipsies dance; Zuniga is talking to her softly, but she is ignoring him. Suddenly she gets up and begins to sing.

Scene One. *Carmen, Zuniga, Andres and other Officers and Gipsies. / No. 11 Gipsy Song*

CARMEN

I

The triangles they used to play   [15]
Would set the gipsy rhythms tingling,
Till roused by their metallic jingling
The gipsy girls began to sway.
Their tambourines took up the theme,

While mad guitars in rhythm beating
Were unrelentingly repeating
This very song, this same refrain!
Tra, la, la, la, la, la, la.

Les tringles des sistres tintaient
Avec un éclat métallique,
Et sur cette étrange musique
Les zingarellas se levaient.
Tambours de basque allaient leur train,

Et les guitares forcenées
Grinçaient sous des mains obstinées,
Même chanson, même refrain!
Tra, la, la, la, la, la, la.

The gipsies dance during the refrain. Mercedes and Frasquita join in the chorus with Carmen.

II

The copper and the silver rings
Would shine against the dusky faces;
The red and orange of their dresses
Would go swirling upon the wind;
And soon the dance was under way.
It started slowly with the singing,
Then gaining speed and wildly
   spinning,
It whirled away, away, away, away!
Tra, la, la, la, la, la, la.

Les anneaux de cuivre et d'argent
Reluisaient sur les peaux bistrées;
D'orange et de rouge zébrées
Les étoffes flottaient au vent;
La danse au chant se mariait,
D'abord indécise et timide,
Plus vive ensuite et plus rapide,

Cela montait, montait, montait!
Tra, la, la, la, la, la, la.

MERCEDES AND FRASQUITA

Tra, la, la, la, la, la, la.

Tra, la, la, la, la, la, la.

CARMEN

III

The gipsy men with hands awhirl,
Beat out a rhythm mad, demonic,
Intoxicating with their music
Inflaming every gipsy girl!
And by the rhythm of the song,
Demented and with passion burning,
They were swept away, wildly turning,
In a whirlwind borne along!
Tra, la, la, la, la, la, la.

Les Bohémiennes à tour de bras,
De leurs instruments faisaient rage,
Et cet éblouissant tapage
Ensorcelait les zingaras!
Sous le rythme de la chanson,
Ardentes, folles, enfiévrées,
Elles se laissaient, enivrées,
Emporter par le tourbillon!
Tra, la, la, la, la, la, la.

ALL THREE

Tra, la, la, la, la, la, la.

Tra, la, la, la, la, la, la.

The dance grows very fast and passionate. Carmen dances too and falls onto a bench breathless as the last notes of the orchestra die away. Lillas Pastia now begins to hover round the officers, rather embarrassed.

ZUNIGA

What is it, Lillas Pastia?

Vous avez quelque chose à nous dire, maître Lillas Pastia?

	PASTIA
Señores . . .	Mon Dieu, Messieurs . . .
	ANDRES
Come on, out with it . . .	Parle, voyons . . .
	PASTIA
It's getting late . . . and I, in particular, am obliged to obey the regulations as I am not in the Magistrates' good books . . . I can't think why . . .	Il commence à se faire tard . . . et je suis, plus que personne, obligé d'observer les règlements. Monsieur le corrégidor étant assez mal disposé à mon égard . . . je ne sais pas pourquoi il est mal disposé . . .
	ZUNIGA
I know damned well why! . . . All the smugglers of the province meet at your inn.	Je le sais très bien, moi. C'est parce que ton auberge est le rendez-vous ordinaire de tous les contrebandiers de la province.
	PASTIA
Well, whatever the reason, I have to take care . . . and it's getting very late.	Que ce soit pour cette raison ou pour un autre, je suis obligé de prendre garde . . . or, je vous le répète, il commence à se faire tard.
	ANDRES
That means you want to throw us out!	Cela veut dire que tu nous mets à la porte!
	PASTIA
Oh no, Señores! . . . oh no! . . . I only wanted to draw your attention to the fact that I should have closed ten minutes ago . . .	Oh! non, messieurs les officiers . . . oh! non . . . je vous fais seulement observer que mon auberge devrait être fermée depuis dix minutes . . .
	ZUNIGA
God knows what goes on here once you *are* closed . . .	Dieu sait ce qui s'y passe dans ton auberge, une fois qu'elle est fermée . . .
	PASTIA
Lieutenant!	Oh! mon lieutenant . . .
	ZUNIGA
Well, we've still time for an hour at the theatre. You're coming with us, girls, aren't you?	Enfin, nous avons encore, avant l'appel, le temps d'aller passer une heure au théâtre . . . vous y viendrez avec nous, n'est-ce pas, les belles?

(*Pastia makes signs to the girls to refuse.*)

	FRASQUITA
No, Señores, no, we're staying here.	Non, messieurs les officiers, non, nous restons ici, nous.
	ZUNIGA
What, you're not coming?	Comment, vous ne viendrez pas . . .
	MERCEDES
It's impossible . . .	C'est impossible.
	ANDRES
Mercedes! . . .	Mercédès! . . .
	MERCEDES
I'm sorry . . .	Je regrette . . .
	ANDRES
Frasquita! . . .	Frasquita! . . .

I'm heartbroken . . .

Je suis désolée . . .

ZUNIGA

But Carmen, I'm sure *you* won't refuse . . .

Mais toi, Carmen, je suis bien sûr que tu ne refuseras pas . . .

CARMEN

That's just where you are wrong, Lieutenant . . . I *do* refuse, [even more flatly, if possible, than they do . . .]

C'est ce qui vous trompe, mon lieutenant . . . je refuse et encore plus nettement qu'elles deux, si c'est possible . . .

Whilst Zuniga is talking to Carmen, Andres and the other officers try to persuade Frasquita and Mercedes.

ZUNIGA

Don't you like me?

Tu m'en veux?

CARMEN

Why shouldn't I like you?

Pourquoi vous en voudrais-je?

ZUNIGA

Because a month ago [I was brute enough to send] I sent you to prison . . .

Parce qu'il y a un mois, j'ai eu la cruauté de t'envoyer à la prison . . .

CARMEN
(as if she didn't remember)

To prison?

A la prison?

ZUNIGA

I was on duty: I couldn't do anything else.

J'étais de service, je ne pouvais pas faire autrement.

CARMEN
(as before)

[To prison . . .] I don't remember going to prison . . .

A la prison . . . je ne me souviens pas d'être allée à la prison . . .

ZUNIGA

I know damned well you didn't go! . . . The Corporal who was taking you [thought fit to] let you escape and got himself demoted and imprisoned for it . . .

Je sais pardieu bien que tu n'y es pas allée . . . le brigadier qui était chargé de te conduire ayant jugé à propos de te laisser échapper . . . et de se faire dégrader et emprisonner pour cela . . .

CARMEN
(seriously)

[Demoted and imprisoned?

Dégrader et imprisonner? . . .

ZUNIGA

Good God, yes . . . One doesn't like to admit that such a charming little hand was strong enough to push over a grown man . . .

Mon Dieu oui . . . on n'a pas voulu admettre qu'une aussi petite main ait été assez forte pour renverser un homme . . .

CARMEN

Oh!

Oh!

ZUNIGA

It just didn't seem natural . . .

Cela n'a pas paru naturel . . .

CARMEN

And this poor boy is now just a private again?

Et ce pauvre garçon est redevenu simple soldat?

ZUNIGA

Yes . . . and he spent a month in prison . . .]

Oui . . . et il a passé un mois en prison . . .

But is he out yet?

Mais il en est sorti?

ZUNIGA

He came out today.*

Depuis hier seulement!

CARMEN
(*clicking her castanets*)

Well that's fine, if he's out, that's fine!

Tout est bien, puisqu'il en est sorti, tout est bien.

ZUNIGA

[Good Heavens! You've got over it quickly ...

A la bonne heure, tu te consoles vite ...

CARMEN
(*aside*)

Naturally! ...

Et j'ai raison ...
(*aloud*)

If you take my advice, you'll do as I do ... you want to take us out, we don't want to go ... you'll get over it! ...

Si vous m'en croyez, vous ferez comme moi, vous voulez nous emmener, nous ne voulons pas vous suivre ... vous vous consolerez ...

ANDRES

We'll have to.]

Il faudra bien.

The scene is interrupted by the sound of the Chorus from the wings. / No. 12 Chorus and Ensemble.

CHORUS

Hurrah! Long live the Torero!
Hurrah! Long live Escamillo!
Oh never did Torero
With such unerring hand,
And a blow that was fairer,
Fell the bull to the ground!
Hurrah! Long live the Torero!
Hurrah! Long live Escamillo!

Vivat! vivat le torero!
Vivat! vivat Escamillo!
Jamais homme intrépide
N'a, par un coup plus beau,
D'une main plus rapide
Terrassé le taureau!
Vivat! vivat le torero!
Vivat! vivat Escamillo!

ZUNIGA
(*over music of offstage chorus*)

What's all that about?

Qu'est-ce que c'est que ça?

MERCEDES

A torchlight procession.

Une promenade aux flambeaux ...

ANDRES

And who are they cheering?

Et qui promène-t-on?

FRASQUITA

I know him ... it's Escamillo ... the torero who's made his name in Grenada [and who promises to become as renowned as Montes and Pepo Illo ...

Je le reconnais ... c'est Escamillo ... un torero qui s'est fait remarquer aux dernières courses de Grenade et qui promet d'égaler la gloire de Montes et de Pepo Illo ...

ANDRES

I say! We must make him come in here, and drink to him.]

Pardieu, il faut le faire venir ... nous boirons en son honneur!

ZUNIGA

Right! I'll go and invite him.

C'est cela, je vais l'inviter.
(*He goes to the window.*)

Señor Torero ... would you come in and

Monsieur le torero ... voulez-vous nous

---

* hier: but see p. 93, José: I've only been out of prison two hours.

join us?You'll find people here who admire skill and courage like yours!	faire l'amitié de monter ici? Vous y trouverez des gens qui aiment fort tous ceux qui, comme vous, ont de l'adresse et du courage ...

(coming back into the room)

He's coming ...	Il vient ...

PASTIA
(pleading)

Señores, please ... I have told you ...	Messieurs les officiers, je vous avais dit ...

ZUNIGA

[Have the goodness to leave us alone, Lillas Pastia, and bring us something to drink ...]	Ayez la bonté de nous laisser tranquille, maître Lillas Pastia, et faites-nous apporter de quoi boire ...

CHORUS

Hurrah! Long live the Torero! Hurrah! Long live Escamillo!	Vivat! vivat le torero! Vivat! vivat Escamillo!

(Escamillo appears.)

Scene Two. *The Same, Escamillo / No. 15 Couplets*

ZUNIGA

[Señor Torero, these ladies and we ourselves would like to thank you for accepting our invitation; we don't want to let you go past before] we drink to you and to the great art of bull-fighting.	Ces dames et nous, vous remercions d'avoir accepté notre invitation; nous n'avons pas voulu vous laisser passer sans boire avec vous au grand art de la tauromachie.

ESCAMILLO

Señores, I thank you.	Messieurs les officiers, je vous remercie.

I
[16] †

To your toast, I now drink another, Señor, señor, to this I have the right, For we Toreros all are your brothers Your real joy in life, like ours, is the fight. The arena's full, the day a Fiesta.	Votre toast ... je peux vous le rendre, Señors, señors car avec les soldats Oui, les toreros peuvent s'entendre: Pour plaisirs, pour plaisirs, ils ont les combats. Le cirque est plein, c'est jour de fête.
The arena's full, they're herded tight: The noisy crowd, past all restraining, Lashing themselves to a frenzy yell with delight; Rowdy taunting, with shouts and jeering, Making passions hot and tempers rise! Today's the day we prove our daring; And the day that the brave will prize. Come on, on guard. Ah! ...	Le cirque est plein, du haut en bas. Les spectateurs, perdant la tête, Les spectateurs s'interpellent à grand fracas; Apostrophes, cris et tapage Poussés jusques à la fureur, Car c'est la fête du courage, C'est la fête des gens de cœur. Allons! en garde. Ah! ...

(pleased with himself)

Toreador, on guard now, Toreador, Toreador! Do not forget that when you draw your sword *Two dark eyes look down And love is your reward.	Toreador, en garde! Toreador! Toreador! Et songe, bien, oui, songe en combattant *Qu'un œil noir te regarde Et que l'amour t'attend.

(Carmen fills Escamillo's glass.)

---

† When Bizet composed these couplets he re-wrote some words and half lines in a different order to make the story more dramatic and less conventional.

* In the novel Carmen often covered one eye with her Mantilla.

All at once the crowd is silent: The crowd is silent, whatever's happening? More shouting! Here he comes! Look, the bull is free And rushing out into the ring ... In he bounds and then he charges, a horse goes rolling With him goes a picador. 'Ah, Bravo toro!' bellow the people. Off goes the bull, then turns ready to gore! He tries to shake the banderillas off ... And charges on enraged, the blood is flowing fast! Off they run, try to climb the barriers! Now it's your turn at last. Come on, on guard. Ah! Toreador, on guard now, Toreador, Toreador! Do not forget that when you draw your sword Two dark eyes look down And love is your reward.	Tout d'un coup, on fait silence, On fait silence ... Ah! que se passe-t-il? Plus de cris, c'est l'instant! le taureau s'élance En bondissant hors du toril ... Il s'élance! il entre, il frappe! ... un cheval roule En entraînant un picador. Ah, Bravo! Toro! hurle la foule. Le taureau va, il vient, et frappe encore! En secouant ses banderilles ... Plein de fureur, il court! le cirque est plein de sang! On se sauve, on franchit les grilles! ... C'est ton tour maintenant. Allons! en garde! Ah! Toreador, en garde! Toreador! Toreador! Et songe bien, oui, songe en com- battant Qu'un œil noir te regarde Et que l'amour t'attend.

ALL

Toreador, on guard now! (*etc.*)	Toreador, en garde. (*etc.*)

(*Everyone drinks and shakes Escamillo's hand.*)

PASTIA

Señores, I beg you ...	Messieurs les officiers, je vous en prie.

ZUNIGA

Alright, alright! We're going.	C'est bien, c'est bien, nous partons.

(*The officers get ready to go. Escamillo is near Carmen.*)

ESCAMILLO

Tell me your name, [and the next time I kill a bull, that name will be on my lips.	Dis-moi ton nom, et la première fois que je frapperai le taureau, ce sera ton nom que je prononcerai.

CARMEN

My name's Carmencita.]	Je m'appelle la Carmencita.

ESCAMILLO

Carmencita?	La Carmencita?

CARMEN

[Carmencita] — or Carmen, as you like.	Carmen, la Carmencita, comme tu voudras.

ESCAMILLO

[Very well, Carmen or Carmencita] if I should presume to love you, and want to be loved by you, what would you say?	Eh bien! Carmen ou la Carmencita, si je m'avisais de t'aimer et d'être aimé de toi, qu'est-ce que tu me répondrais?

CARMEN

I'd say love me as much as you like, but as to *my* loving *you*, just now that's out of the question ...	Je répondrais que tu peux m'aimer tout à ton aise, mais que quant à être aimé de moi pour le moment, il ne faut pas y songer!

ESCAMILLO

Ah!   Ah!

CARMEN

[That's how it is.]   C'est comme ça.

ESCAMILLO

Then I'll wait and be content to hope ...   J'attendrais alors et je me contenterai
                                   d'espérer ...

CARMEN

There's no ban on waiting, and it's always   Il n'est pas défendu d'attendre et il est
pleasant to hope.   toujours agréable d'espérer.

ANDRES
(*to Frasquita and Mercedes*)

You're really not coming?   Vous ne venez pas décidément?

FRASQUITA AND MERCEDES
(*as Pastia signals again*)

No, no: impossible.   Mais non, mais non ...

ANDRES
(*to Zuniga*)

It's a losing battle!   Mauvais campagne, lieutenant.

ZUNIGA

Nonsense! The battle's not yet lost ...   Bah! La bataille n'est pas encore
                                   perdue ...
              (*softly to Carmen*)
Listen Carmen, as you won't come with   Écoute-moi, Carmen, puisque tu ne veux
us, I'll be back here in an hour ...   pas venir avec nous, c'est moi qui dans
                                   une heure reviendrai ici ...

CARMEN

[Here?   Ici?

ZUNIGA

Yes, in an hour ... after roll-call.]   Oui, dans une heure ... après l'appel.

CARMEN

I don't advise you to come back ...   Je ne vous conseille pas de revenir ...

ZUNIGA
(*laughing*)

I shall come all the same.   Je reviendrai tout de même.
               (*aloud*)
We'll go with you Torero, and join your   Nous partons avec vous, torero, et nous
procession.   nous joindrons au cortège qui vous
                                   accompagne.

ESCAMILLO

That's a great honour. And I hope I shall   C'est un grand honneur pour moi, je
not prove unworthy next time you see me   tâcherai de ne pas m'en montrer indigne
fight.   lorsque je combattrai sous vos yeux.

[13b]

CHORUS

Toreador, on guard now!   [17]   Toreador, en garde,
     (*etc.*)   (*etc.*)

They all go off leaving Carmen, Frasquita, Mercedes and Lillas Pastia onstage.

Scene Three.

FRASQUITA
(to Pastia)

[Why in such a hurry to get rid of them and] why did you make signs to us not to go?

Pourquoi étais-tu si pressé de les faire partir et pourquoi nous as-tu fait signe de ne pas les suivre?

PASTIA

Dancairo and Remendado have arrived!... [They want to talk business, Egyptian business.]

Le Dancaïre et le Remendado viennent d'arriver... ils ont à vous parler de vos affaires, des affaires d'Egypte.

CARMEN

Dancairo and Remendado?...

Le Dancaïre et le Remendado?...

PASTIA
(He opens a door and beckons them in.)

Yes, here they are... hang on!...

Oui, les voici... tenez...

(Pastia bolts the doors and the shutters.)

Scene Four. *Carmen, Frasquita, Mercedes, Dancairo, Remendado.*

FRASQUITA

[Well,] what's the news?

Eh bien, les nouvelles?

DANCAIRO

Not bad!... just come from Gibraltar...

Pas trop mauvaises les nouvelles; nous arrivons de Gibraltar...

REMENDADO

Nice place Gibraltar!... Full of Englishmen... Handsome men, the English — a bit cold, but so elegant...

Jolie ville, Gibraltar!... on y voit des Anglais, de jolis hommes les Anglais; un peu froids, mais distingués.

DANCAIRO

Remendado!...

Remendado!...

REMENDADO

Yes, boss?

Patron.

DANCAIRO
(putting a hand on his knife)

You understand?

Vous comprenez?

REMENDADO

Perfectly, boss!

Parfaitement, patron...

DANCAIRO

Then shut up! [We've just come from Gibraltar.] We've [arranged with a ship's captain for the shipment of] a cargo of English merchandise which we'll await near the coast. We'll hide some in the mountains... the rest we'll smuggle through. Our people have been warned... [They are in hiding]. But it's you three girls we need... [you're coming with us...]

Taisez-vous alors. Nous arrivons de Gibraltar, nous avons arrangé, avec un patron de navire, l'embarquement des marchandises anglaises. Nous irons les attendre près de la côte, nous en cacherons une partie dans la montagne et nous ferons passer le reste. Tous nos camarades ont été prévenus... ils sont ici, cachés, mais c'est de vous trois surtout que nous avons besoin... vous allez partir avec nous...

CARMEN
(laughing)

What for? To help you carry the bales?

Pour quoi faire? Pour vous aider à porter des ballots?...

87

REMENDADO

Oh no!... The ladies carry the bales ... that's not very elegant!	On! non ... faire porter des ballots à des dames ... ça ne serait pas distingué.

DANCAIRO
(*menacingly*)

Remendado?	Remendado?

REMENDADO

Yes, boss.	Oui, Patron.

DANCAIRO

We won't make you carry the bales, we need you for something else.	Nous ne vous ferons pas porter de ballots, mais nous avons besoin de vous pour autre chose.

No. 14 Quintet

DANCAIRO

We've a little plan, very clever!	[18]	Nous avons en tête une affaire.

MERCEDES, FRASQUITA

And one that it will pay to do?	Est-elle bonne, dites-nous?

DANCAIRO, REMENDADO

Never knew a better, no never; But now we need some help from you.	Elle est admirable, ma chère; Mais nous avons besoin de vous!

ALL THREE WOMEN

You do?	De nous?

BOTH MEN

We do. For we most humbly beg to state, And most respectfully of course, When you have dirty work in view, Anything new, Tricky to do, Nothing is easier, we have found, Given a few women around, But without The beauty about, We never seem to do So well!	De vous! Car nous l'avouons humblement, Et fort respectueusement, Quand il s'agit de tromperie, De duperie, De volerie, Il est toujours bon, sur ma foi, D'avoir les femmes avec soi. Et sans elles, Mes toutes belles, On ne fait jamais rien De bien!

ALL THREE WOMEN

What, without us never Do well?	Quoi! sans nous jamais rien, De bien?

BOTH MEN

With that we know you will agree?	N'êtes-vous pas de cet avis?

ALL THREE WOMEN

You're right, with that We quite agree.	Si fait, je suis De cet avis.

ALL FIVE

When you have dirty work in view, [19] Anything new, Tricky to do, Nothing is easier, we have found, Given a few women around. But without The beauty about We never seem to do So well!	Quand il s'agit de tromperie, De duperie, De volerie, Il est toujours bon, sur ma foi, D'avoir les femmes avec soi. Et sans elles, Les toutes belles, On ne fait jamais rien De bien!

Agreed, and so you leave today.   C'est dit, alors; vous partirez?

MERCEDES, FRASQUITA

Just when you say.   Quand vous voudrez.

REMENDADO

Now, right away.   Mais tout de suite.

CARMEN

Ah! If I may, let me say;   Ah! permettez, permettez!
(to Mercedes and Frasquita)
If you want to be off — away!   S'il vous plaît de partir, partez!
But you won't find me in the party.   Mais je ne suis pas du voyage.
I will not go ... I will not go!   Je ne pars pas ... je ne pars pas.

DANCAIRO

Carmen, my darling, you must go.   Carmen, mon amour, tu viendras,
You wouldn't surely have the heart   Et tu n'auras pas le courage
To stay and leave us in the cart!   De nous laisser dans l'embarras.

MERCEDES, FRASQUITA

Ah! But Carmen, say you'll go!   Ah! ma Carmen tu viendras!

CARMEN

I tell you no! I tell you no!   Je ne pars pas, je ne pars pas!

DANCAIRO

But at least tell us why, Carmen, you   Mais, au moins, la raison, Carmen, tu la
answer no!   diras?

THE OTHER FOUR

Tell us why, tell us why, tell us why, tell us   La raison, la raison, la raison, la raison!
why!

CARMEN

Oh yes, of course I'll tell you why;   Je la dirai certainement;

THE OTHER FOUR

Go on, go on, go on, go on!   Voyons, voyons, voyons, voyons!

CARMEN

The reason is just now that I ...   La raison, c'est qu'en ce moment ...

THE OTHER FOUR

Go on, go on, go on, go on!   Eh bien, eh bien, eh bien, eh bien!

CARMEN

...find I am in love ...!   ... je suis amoureuse.

BOTH MEN
(astounded)

What did she say?   Qu'a-t-elle dit?

BOTH WOMEN

She said she finds herself in love!   Elle dit qu'elle est amoureuse!

BOTH MEN

She's in love!   Amoureuse!

BOTH WOMEN

She's in love!   Amoureuse!

CARMEN

Yes, I'm in love!   Oui, amoureuse!

BOTH MEN

Good Lord, Carmen, try to be serious.   Voyons, Carmen, sois sérieuse.

I'm in love, insanely in love. | Amoureuse à perdre l'esprit.

BOTH MEN

Well we must say we are astonished, [20]
But this won't be the only time
That you, my clever girl, have managed
So as to bring your duty and love into
line.

La chose, certes, nous étonne,
Mais ce n'est pas le premier jour
Où vous aurez su, ma mignonne,
Faire marcher de front le devoir et
l'amour.

CARMEN
(*frankly*)

My friends I'm flattered you should
choose me
To go along with you this time;
This evening though if you'll excuse
me,
Love comes first, duty next, duty and
love won't combine.
This evening, duty and love won't combine.

Mes amis, je serais fort aise
De partir avec vous ce soir
Mais cette foi, ne vous déplaise,
Il faudra que l'amour passe avant le
devoir.
Ce soir l'amour passe avant le devoir!

DANCAIRO

This cannot be your final word? | Ce n'est pas là ton dernier mot?

CARMEN

Oh, yes it is! | Absolument!

REMENDADO

Be kind to us
And change your mind, my dear.

Il faut
Que tu te laisses attendrir.

ALL FOUR

You must be there, Carmen, you
must be there!
For this affair
You must be there;
You know it's true . . .

Il faut venir, Carmen, il faut venir!
Pour notre affaire,
C'est nécessaire;
Car entre nous . . .

CARMEN

Oh, as to that, I quite agree with you. | Quant à cela, j'admets bien avec vous:

ALL FIVE

When you have dirty work in view,
Anything new,
Tricky to do,
Nothing is easier, we have found,
Given a few women around.
But without
The beauty about,
We never seem to do
So well!

Quand il s'agit de tromperie,
De duperie,
De volerie,
Il est toujours bon, sur ma foi,
D'avoir les femmes avec soi,
Et sans elles,
Les toutes belles,
On ne fait jamais rien
De bien!

DANCAIRO

That's enough; I've said you're to come
and you're coming . . . I'm the boss . . .

En voilà assez; je t'ai dit qu'il fallait venir,
et tu viendras . . . je suis le chef . . .

CARMEN

What did you say? | Comment dis-tu ça?

DANCAIRO

I said I'm the boss . . . | Je te dis que je suis le chef . . .

CARMEN

And you think I'll obey you? . . . | Et tu crois que je t'obéirai? . . .

DANCAIRO
(furious)

Carmen! ...   Carmen! ...

CARMEN
(very calm)

[Well? ...]   Eh bien! ...

REMENDADO
(intervening)

Please, I beg you ... such elegant people ...   Je vous en prie ... des personnes si
                                                 distinguées. ...

DANCAIRO
(aiming a kick which Remendado avoids)

[Get out! ...   Attrape ça, toi ...

REMENDADO
(pulling himself up to his full height)

Boss ...   Patron ...

DANCAIRO

What is it?   Qu'est-ce que c'est?

REMENDADO

Nothing, boss!   Rien, patron!

DANCAIRO
(to Carmen)

In love ... that's not a reason.   Amoureuse ... ce n'est pas une raison,
                                              cela.

REMENDADO

As a matter of fact you're not the only   Le fait est que ce n'en est pas une ... moi
one ... I'm in love too but that doesn't   aussi je suis amoureux et ça ne m'empêche
prevent me making myself useful!]   pas de me rendre utile.

CARMEN

Go without me ... I'll join you   Partez sans moi ... j'irai vous rejoindre
tomorrow ... tonight I'm staying.   demain, mais pour ce soir je reste ...

FRASQUITA

I've never seen you like this before: who   Je ne t'ai jamais vue comme cela; qui
ever are you expecting? ...   attends-tu donc?

CARMEN

A [poor devil of a] soldier who's done me a Un pauvre diable de soldat qui m'a rendu
service.   service.

MERCEDES

The one who went to prison?   Ce soldat qui était en prison?

CARMEN

Yes.   Oui.

FRASQUITA

The one you sent a loaf of bread to [by the Et à qui, il y a quinze jours, le geôlier a
jailor a fortnight ago], with a gold coin and remis de ta part un pain dans lequel il y
a file in it?   avait une pièce d'or et une lime? ...

CARMEN
(going back towards the window)

Yes.   Oui.

DANCAIRO

Did he use the file?   Il s'en est servi de cette lime? ...

No.   Non.

DANCAIRO

You see! Your soldier was afraid [of being punished even more harshly than he had been already]; and he'll be afraid this evening too ... [it's a waste of time, opening the shutters to look for him.] I bet you he won't come.

Tu vois bien! Ton soldat aura eu peur d'être puni plus rudement qu'il ne l'avait été; ce soir encore il aura peur ... tu auras beau entr'ouvrir les volets et regarder s'il vient, je parierais qu'il ne viendra pas.

CARMEN
(at the window)

Don't bet, you'll lose.   Ne parie pas, tu perdrais ...

Don José's voice can be heard off-stage. / No. 15 Song.

JOSE
(off-stage)

"Hey, hola!   [21]   Halte-là!
Who goes there?"   Qui va là?
"Friend from Alcala!"   Dragon d'Alcala!
"Where are you going there,   Où t'en vas-tu par là,
Friend from Alcala?"   Dragon d'Alcala?
"Off to do some fighting,   Moi je m'en vais faire
Till the foe is writhing,   Mordre la poussière,
And the dust he's biting."   A mon adversaire.
"Well, if that's the case,   S'il en est ainsi,
Soldier, you may pass.   Passez mon ami,
When it's for a fight,   Affaire d'honneur,
Or affair of the heart   Affaire de cœur;
We will never bar   Pour nous tout est là,
Friends from Alcala!"   Dragons d'Alcala.

The music continues. Through the half-open shutters, Carmen, Dancairo, Remendado, Mercedes and Frasquita watch Don José approach.

MERCEDES

Look it is a Dragoon!   C'est un dragon, ma foi.

FRASQUITA

And a handsome Dragoon!   Et un beau dragon.

DANCAIRO
(to Carmen)

Well, as you refuse to come till tomorrow, [the least you can do is ...

Eh bien, puisque tu ne veux venir que demain, sais-tu au moins ce que tu devrais faire?

CARMEN

What?]   Qu'est-ce que je devrais faire?

DANCAIRO

... persuade your soldier to join us.

Tu devrais décider ton dragon à venir avec toi et à se joindre à nous.

CARMEN

[Ah! ... if only I could! ... But it's nonsense even to think of it ...] He's too innocent ...

Ah! ... si cela se pouvait! ... mais il n'y faut pas penser ... Ce sont des bêtises ... il est trop niais.

DANCAIRO

Then why do you love him, [if you think that?

Pourquoi l'aimes-tu puisque tu en conviens toi-même?

CARMEN

Because he looks nice and I like him.

Parce qu'il est joli garçon donc et qu'il me plaît.

The boss doesn't understand that you've only to be a nice-looking boy for the girls to run after you ...	Le patron ne comprend pas ça, lui ... qu'il suffise d'être joli garçon pour plaire aux femmes ...

DANCAIRO

[Just you wait! ...]	Attends un peu, toi, attends un peu ...

Remendado runs off, Dancairo chases him, followed by Mercedes and Frasquita who try to calm him.

JOSE
(*in the distance, gradually approaching*)

"Hey, hola!	Halte-là!
Who goes there?"	Qui va là?
"Friend from Alcala!"	Dragon d'Alcala?
"Where are you going there,	Où t'en vas-tu par là,
Friend from Alcala?"	Dragon d'Alcala?
"Punctual you see me,	Exact et fidèle,
Faithful to my duty	Je vais où m'appelle
At the call of beauty!"	L'amour de ma belle.
"Well, if that's the case,	S'il en est ainsi,
Soldier you may pass.	Passez mon ami.
When it's for a fight	Affaire d'honneur,
Or affair of the heart,	Affaire de cœur,
We will never bar	Pour nous tout est là,
Friends from Alcala!"	Dragons d'Alcala!

(*Enter Don José.*)

Scene Five. *Don José, Carmen*

CARMEN

At last ... you're here ... I'm glad!	Enfin ... te voilà ... C'est bien heureux!

JOSE

I've only been out of prison a couple of hours.	Il y a deux heures seulement que je suis sorti de prison.

CARMEN

What stopped you getting out before? I sent you a file and a gold coin ... The file was to cut through your prison bars ... and a gold coin for the nearest old clothes shop to exchange your uniform for civilian clothes.	Qui t'empêchait de sortir plus tôt? Je t'avais envoyé une lime et une pièce d'or ... avec la lime il fallait scier le plus gros barreau de ta prison ... avec la pièce d'or il fallait, chez le premier fripier venu, changer ton uniforme pour un habit bourgeois.

JOSE

It was all quite possible ...	En effet, tout cela était possible.

CARMEN

Then why didn't you?	Pourquoi ne l'as-tu pas fait?

JOSE

Well? I still have my honour as a soldier. It would be criminal to desert ... Oh! but I'm grateful to you none the less ... You sent me a file and a gold coin ... I shall keep the file to sharpen my lance and to remind me of you.	Que veux-tu? J'ai encore mon honneur de soldat, et déserter me semblerait un grand crime ... Oh! je ne t'en suis pas moins reconnaissant ... Tu m'as envoyé une lime et une pièce d'or ... La lime me servira pour affiler ma lance et je la garde comme souvenir de toi.

(*giving her the gold coin*)

And the coin ...	Quant à l'argent ...

CARMEN

You've still got it! ... It's incredible! ...	Tiens, il l'a gardé! ... ça se trouve à merveille ...

(shouting and clapping her hands)

Hey!... Lillas Pastia!   Holà!... Lillas Pastia, holà!...

(to José)

We'll eat the lot... You shall treat   Nous mangerons tout... tu me régales...
me... Hey! Come here!   holà! holà!

(Enter Pastia.)

PASTIA
(trying to quieten her)

Do be careful!   Prenez donc garde...

CARMEN
(throwing Pastia the coin)

Here! Catch!... bring us crystallised   Tiens, attrappe... et apporte-nous des
fruit... and sweets and oranges and   fruits confits; apporte-nous des bonbons,
manzanilla... bring us everything   apporte-nous des oranges, apporte-nous
you've got, everything...   du Manzanilla... apporte-nous de tout
     ce que tu as, de tout, de tout...

PASTIA

Immediately, Señorita Carmencita.   Tout de suite, mademoiselle Carmencita.
(Exit.)

CARMEN
(to José)

You're cross with me then, and sorry you   Tu m'en veux alors et tu regrettes de
went to prison for the sake of my   t'être fait mettre en prison pour mes
beautiful eyes?   beaux yeux?

JOSE

As a matter of fact, I'm not!   Quant à cela non, par exemple.

CARMEN

[Really?   Vraiment?

JOSE

I have been in prison and I've been   L'on m'a mis en prison, l'on m'a ôté mon
downgraded, but I don't care.]   grade, mais ça m'est égal.

CARMEN

Because you love me?   Parce que tu m'aimes?

JOSE

Because I love you, because I adore you.   Oui, parce que je t'aime, parce que je
     t'adore.

CARMEN
(putting her hands in his)

I pay my debts... that's gipsy law... I   Je paie mes dettes... c'est notre loi à
pay my debts... I pay my debts...   nous autres bohémiennes... Je paie mes
     dettes... je paie mes dettes...

(Lillas Pastia returns with a dish of oranges, sweets, crystallised fruits and Manzanilla.)

Put it down here... [the whole lot...   Mets tout cela ici... d'un seul coup,
don't be afraid...   n'aie pas peur...

(Pastia obeys and half the things fall onto the floor.)

That doesn't matter, we'll pick it up   Ça ne fait rien, nous ramasserons tout
later...]Go on, run away now, run   cela nous-mêmes... sauve-toi maintenant,
away.   sauve-toi, sauve-toi.

(Exit Pastia.)

You sit here and we'll eat it all! All! All!   Mets-toi là et mangeons de tout! de tout!
     de tout!

(She sits and Don José sits opposite her.)

JOSE

[You munch sweets like a child of six ...	Tu croques les bonbons comme un enfant de six ans ...

CARMEN

... because I like them] ... Your lieutenant was here just now with some other officers. They made us dance ...	C'est que je les aime ... Ton lieutenant était ici tout à l'heure, avec d'autres officiers, ils nous ont fait danser la Romalis† ...

JOSE

And you danced?	Tu as dansé?

CARMEN

Yes; and when I'd danced, your lieutenant said he adored me ...	Oui; et quand j'ai eu dansé, ton lieutenant s'est permis de me dire qu'il m'adorait ...

JOSE

Carmen!	Carmen!

CARMEN

What's the matter? Are you jealous [by any chance?	Qu'est-ce que tu as? ... Est-ce que tu serais jaloux, pas hasard? ...

JOSE

Of course I'm jealous ...	Mais certainement, je suis jaloux ...

CARMEN

Good! ... Go on! You canary ... you are a real canary in coat* and character ... now don't get ruffled ... why so jealous ... because I danced for those officers? ...] Alright, now I'll dance for you if you like ... just for you ...	Ah bien! ... Canari, va! ... tu es un vrai canari d'habit et de caractère ... Allons, ne te fâche pas ... Pourquoi es-tu jaloux? Parce que j'ai dansé tout à l'heure pour ces officiers ... Eh bien, si tu veux, je danserai pour toi maintenant, pour toi seul.

JOSE

[If I like ... I certainly do like ...]	Si je le veux, je crois bien que je le veux ...

CARMEN

Where are my castanets? ... What have I done with my castanets? ...	Où sont mes castagnettes? ... Qu'est-ce que j'ai fait de mes castagnettes? ...

(laughing)

[You must have taken them!	C'est toi qui me les a prises, mes castagnettes?

JOSE

I haven't!	Mais non!

CARMEN
(tenderly)

You have; you have; I'm sure you have ... [Oh, well, these will do.	Mais si, mais si ... je suis sûr que c'est toi ... ah bah! en voilà des castagnettes.

(She breaks a plate and makes two castanets from the pieces of pottery and tries them.)

Oh! They'll never be as good as my real castanets] ... Where are they?	Ah! ça ne vaudra jamais mes castagnettes ... Où sont-elles donc?

JOSE
(seeing the castanets on a table on the right)

Here they are ...	Tiens, les voici ...

---

† The Romalis was a very old and sexy gipsy dance.

* The Dragoons wore a yellow uniform.

CARMEN
(laughing)

There, you see! . . . it *was* you [who took them]! . . .

Ah! Tu vois bien . . . c'est toi qui les avais prises . . .

JOSE

Carmen, I love you, I adore you!

Ah! que je t'aime, Carmen, que je t'aime!

CARMEN

[I should hope so!]

Je l'espère bien.

No. 16 Duet

CARMEN
(gaily)

Now I will dance only for you,
   And you will see, my lord . . .
How I can make the music I need for my dancing.

Je vais danser en votre honneur,
   Et vous verrez, seigneur,
Comment je sais moi-même accompagner ma danse.

(with mock solemnity)

So take your seat, Don José. We are starting!

[22] Mettez-vous là, Don José, je commence!

She makes Don José sit down. Dancing and humming she accompanies herself on the castanets. Don José watches her, entranced. Soon in the distance the sound of bugles is heard. Don José listens. He thinks he might have heard the bugles but Carmen's castanets click so loudly that he is not sure. Don José goes up to Carmen and takes her by the arms, forcing her to stop.

JOSE

Please will you stop, Carmen, please will you stop a moment.

Attends un peu, Carmen, rien qu'un moment, arrête.

CARMEN
(astonished)

And what for, may I ask?

Et pourquoi, s'il te plaît?

JOSE

      I am certain, out there . . .
Yes, there goes the retreat, I hear our bugles calling . . .
   Can you not hear them too?

      Il me semble, là-bas . . .
Oui, ce sont nos clairons qui sonnent la retraite . . .
   Ne les entends-tu pas?

CARMEN
(happily)

Bravo! I've tried my hardest, but nothing's more depressing
Than to dance without music . . . Hurrah then for the music
That has dropped from the blue!

Bravo! j'avais beau faire . . . Il est mélancolique
De danser sans orchestre. Et vive la musique
Qui nous tombe du ciel!

She begins to sing again in rhythm with the bugles off-stage . . . She returns to her dance and Don José to watching her. The sound of the bugles comes nearer . . . nearer . . . passing under the windows of the inn . . . then moves away, becoming fainter and fainter . . . Don José again tries to tear himself away from Carmen . . . He takes her by the arms and forces her to stop once more.

JOSE

But you don't understand, Carmen . . .
   Retreat is sounding!
I must be there for roll-call in barracks tonight!

Tu ne m'as pas compris . . . Carmen c'est la retraite . . .
Il faut que, moi, je rentre au quartier pour l'appel!

(The sound of the bugles stops suddenly.)

CARMEN
(stupefied and looking at Don José, who is putting on his pouch and belt)

Back to barracks! For the night!

Au quartier! Pour l'appel!

Ah! How could I be so stupid!	Ah! j'étais vraiment bien bête!
I tore myself to pieces, no matter what it cost,	Je me mettais en quatre et je faisais des frais
To entertain señor! And I sang! And I danced!	Pour amuser monsieur, je chantais! je dansais!
I thought, Heaven forgive me,	Je crois, Dieu me pardonne,
I was almost in love!	Qu'un peu plus, je l'aimais ...
Ta ra ta ta, my God, there go the bugles!	Ta ra ta ta, c'est le clairon qui sonne!
He's off, he's taken fright!	Il part! Il est parti!
Off you fly, you canary!	Va-t'en donc, canari.

(furiously throwing his cap at him)

Here! take your old cap, your sabre and your pouch too,	Tiens! Prends ton shako, ton sabre, ta giberne.
And get out then, my lad, go on back to your quarters!	Et va-t'en mon garçon, retourne à ta caserne.

JOSE
(sadly)

It's wrong of you, Carmen, to treat me like a fool!	C'est mal à toi, Carmen, de te moquer de moi!
I do not want to go, for up till now no woman,	Je souffre de partir, car jamais, jamais femme,
Till I set eyes on you,	Jamais femme avant toi
No woman yet, till I set eyes on you,	Non, non, jamais, avant toi
Had ever touched my heart and made me care so deeply!	Aussi profondément n'avait troublé mon âme!

CARMEN
(mimicking José's passionate tone)

He does not want to go, for up till now no woman,	† Il souffre de partir, car jamais, jamais femme,
Till he set eyes on me,	Jamais femme avant moi,
No woman yet, till he set eyes on me,	Non, non, jamais avant moi
Had ever touched his heart and made him care so deeply.	Aussi profondément n'avait troublé son âme.
Ta ra ta ta ... "My God there go the bugles!	Ta ra ta ta ... Mon Dieu c'est la retraite!
I am sure I shall be late!" And then he panics! He flies!	Je vais être en retard. Il court, il perd la tête.
There you are! There's his love!	Et voilà son amour!

JOSE

And so you don't believe That I'm in love?	Ainsi tu ne crois pas A mon amour?

CARMEN

Oh no!	Mais non!

JOSE

Alright, now you shall hear.	Eh bien! tu m'entendras!

CARMEN

But I don't want to hear you ...	Je ne veux rien entendre ...
You are keeping them waiting.	Tu vas te faire attendre.

JOSE
(violently)

Hear me you shall! That's enough! Carmen listen to me!	Tu m'entendras, tu m'entendras! Je le veux Carmen, tu m'entendras!

With his left hand he seizes Carmen sharply by the arm, with his right hand he feels inside his tunic for the flower which Carmen threw him in Act One. He shows her the flower.

---

† It was Bizet's idea for Carmen to mock Don José's words.

Here is the flower that you threw me, | La fleur que tu m'avais jetée,
While in the jail it never left me, | Dans ma prison, m'était restée,
Though dry and faded, yet the flower | Flétrie et sèche, cette fleur
Has kept its scent, its magic power; | Gardait toujours sa douce odeur;
In my cell for whole hours together, | Et pendant des heures entières,
I would close my eyes and remember, | Sur mes yeux fermant mes paupières,
Until the scent set me on fire, | De cette odeur je m'enivrais
And in that night I'd see you there! † | Et dans la nuit je te voyais!

Then I would curse the hour I met you, | Je me prenais à te maudire,
And, trying to hate and forget you | A te détester, à me dire:
I'd even say: oh why did fate | Pourquoi faut-il que le destin
Ever decree we two should meet! | L'ait mise là, sur mon chemin?
Then my heart would tell me I wronged you, | Puis je m'accusais de blasphème,
And my only thought was to find you, | Et je ne sentais en moi-même
All that remained was one desire, | Qu'un seul désir, un seul espoir:
Let me find you, Carmen, see you again! | Te revoir, O Carmen, oui, te revoir!...
For you had only to appear there, | Car tu n'avais eu qu'à paraître,
Your dark eyes but to glance my way, | Qu'à jeter un regard sur moi,
And you possessed me then forever, | Pour t'emparer de tout mon être,
O my Carmen! You have enslaved me from that hour! | O ma Carmen! Et j'étais une chose à toi.
Carmen, I love you! | Carmen, je t'aime!

CARMEN

No! You are not in love! | Non! tu ne m'aimes pas!

JOSE

What d'you say? | Que dis-tu?

CARMEN

No! You are not in love! No! No! If it were true, | Non, tu ne m'aimes pas, non, car si tu m'aimais,
Out there, with me, you'd follow too! | Là-bas, là-bas, tu me suivrais!

JOSE

Carmen! | Carmen!

CARMEN
[24]

Yes! into the hills where none would find you, | Oui! Là-bas, là-bas, dans la montagne.
Into the hills we both would ride! | Là-bas, là-bas, tu me suivrais,
Galloping through the countryside, | Sur ton cheval tu me prendrais,
You on your horse with me so close behind you, | Et comme un brave, à travers la campagne,
Carried off, like a gipsy bride! | En croupe tu m'emporterais!

JOSE
(*troubled*)

Carmen! No more! | Carmen! Carmen!

CARMEN

Into the hills where none would find you, | Là-bas, là-bas, dans la montagne
Into the hills we both would ride, | Là-bas, là-bas, tu me suivrais.
We both would ride — were you in love! | Tu me suivrais — si tu m'aimais!
Up there you need answer to no-one; | Tu n'y dépendrais de personne;

---

† Bizet cut the refrain to the first verse.

No orders there, no Captain you need to obey,	Point d'officier à qui tu doives obéir,
Up there no retreat will be sounded,	Et point de retraite qui sonne
Roughly reminding lovers to be on their way!	Pour dire à l'amoureux qu'il est temps de partir!
Sky up above, and open spaces,	Le ciel ouvert, la vie errante;
For one's home all the world, and for law each goes his way!	Pour pays, l'univers; et pour loi, sa volonté!
Best of all, like wine to the senses,	Et surtout la chose enivrante:
The life that's free! The life that's free!	La liberté! La liberté!

DON JOSE
(very shaken)

Oh God! Carmen! Be quiet!	Mon Dieu! Carmen! Tais-toi!

CARMEN

Into the hills, were you in love,	Là-bas, là-bas, dans la montagne,
Into the hills we both would ride!	Là-bas, là-bas, si tu m'aimais,
Into the hills we both would ride!	Là-bas, là-bas, tu me suivrais!
Galloping through the countryside,	Sur ton cheval tu me prendrais
You on your horse with me so close behind you,	Et comme un brave, à travers la campagne,
Just like a gipsy bride, were you in love!	Oui, tu m'emporterais, si tu m'aimais!

JOSE
(almost persuaded)

Carmen! Enough, enough! Be quiet! My God!	Carmen! hélas! tais-toi, mon Dieu!
Carmen! Carmen! Have pity!	Hélas! hélas! pitié!
Carmen have pity!	Carmen, pitié!
Oh my God! Spare me!	O mon Dieu! Hélas!
Ah no more I say!	Ah! tais-toi, tais-toi!

CARMEN

Don't you agree,	Oui, n'est-ce pas,
Into the hills you'll come with me,	Là-bas, là-bas, tu me suivras,
You love me, so you'll come with me.	Tu m'aimes et tu me suivras.
Into the hills take me away!	Là-bas, là-bas, emporte moi.

JOSE
(violently tearing himself away from Carmen's embrace)

No! I will not hear any more!	Non, je ne veux plus t'écouter ...
To leave the Dragoons ... and desert ...	Quitter mon drapeau ... déserter ...
That's dishonour ... and degradation!	C'est la honte, c'est l'infamie!
No, I refuse!	Je n'en veux pas!

CARMEN
(harshly)

Alright! Go!	Eh bien, pars!

JOSE
(begging her)

Carmen, I implore you ...	Carmen, je t'en prie ...

CARMEN

No! My love for you's gone! Go! I detest you!	Non! Je ne t'aime plus! Va! Je te hais!

JOSE

Do listen, Carmen!	Écoute, Carmen!

CARMEN

Goodbye! Don't come near me again.	Adieu! mais adieu pour jamais.

JOSE
(wretchedly)

Alright then, goodbye! Goodbye! And forever!	Eh bien, soit! ... adieu pour jamais.

CARMEN

Get out! . . . Goodbye! Va-t'en . . . Adieu!

JOSE

Carmen! Farewell! Farewell evermore! Carmen! Adieu, adieu pour jamais!

He turns towards the door . . . There is a knock . . . José stops. Silence. Another knock.

Scene Six. *The Same. Zuniga / No. 17 Finale*

ZUNIGA
(outside)

Holà! Carmen! Holà! Holà! Holà! Carmen! holà! holà!

JOSE

Who's knocking? Who is there? Qui frappe? Qui vient là?

CARMEN

Be quiet! Be quiet! Tais-toi! . . . Tais toi!

ZUNIGA
(entering, having forced the door open)

I let myself in my own way. J'ouvre moi-même et j'entre.
(He sees Don José. To Carmen:)

Oh! fie! my beauty! Ah! fi, la belle!
I don't admire your taste! It's stooping Le choix n'est pas heureux; c'est se mésallier
rather low
To choose a common soldier when you De prendre le soldat quand on a l'officier.
might have had me.
(to Don José)
Get out! Clear off now! Allons! Décampe!

JOSE
(calm but determined)

No! Non.

ZUNIGA
(curtly)

Obey! Leave us at once! Si fait, tu partiras.

JOSE

No, I am staying here! Je ne partirai pas.

ZUNIGA
(hitting him across the face)

Insolence! Drôle!

JOSE
(drawing his sword)

How dare you! I'll stand no more from you! Tonnerre! il va pleuvoir des coups!
(Zuniga begins to draw his sabre.)

CARMEN
(dashing between José and Zuniga)
Enough! You jealous fool! Au diable le jaloux!
(calling)
Come on and help! A moi! A moi!

Dancairo, Remendado and the Gipsies appear from all sides. At a sign from Carmen, Dancairo and Remendado disarm Zuniga.

CARMEN
(in a mocking voice to Zuniga)

My fine Señor, it's true Bel officier, l'amour
I fear, that love has played a nasty trick on Vous joue en ce moment un assez vilain
you! tour!
You choose a tactless time Vous arrivez fort mal!

100

At which to re-appear! And so, you force us, we're afraid, Since we don't want to be betrayed, To order you at least . . . an hour's detention.	Vous arrivez fort mal! Hélas! et nous sommes forcés, Ne voulant être dénoncés, De vous garder au moins . . . pendant une heure.

DANCAIRO AND REMENDADO
(very politely to Zuniga, pistols in hand)

My dear Señor, we're going, if we may, to quit this charming mansion. You'll come along with us . . .	Mon cher monsieur, nous allons s'il vous plait, quitter cette demeure; Vous viendrez avec nous . . .

CARMEN
(laughing)

A pleasant little saunter;	C'est une promenade;

DANCAIRO AND REMENDADO

Do you agree? We'd like to have your answer.	Consentez-vous? Répondez, camarade,

ZUNIGA
(taking his part gaily)

Why yes, of course. All the more since you have produced Conclusive arguments to which there is no answer. But you be warned! I'll not forget!	Certainement. D'autant plus que votre argument Est un de ceux auxquels on ne résiste guère! † Mais gare à vous plus tard!

DANCAIRO
(philosophically)

That's too bad! War is war though! So for today, my dear Señor, Just lead the way if you please, to the door!	La guerre, c'est la guerre, En attendant, mon officier, Passez devant sans vous faire prier!

REMENDADO AND CHORUS

Just lead the way, if you please, to the door!	Passez devant sans vous faire prier!

(Zuniga is led out at pistol point by four gipsies.)

CARMEN
(to Don José)

Are you with us? What do you say?	Es-tu des nôtres maintenant?

JOSE
(reluctantly)

I have no choice.	Il le faut bien.

CARMEN

Ah! That's no gallant reply. But who cares though? Come . . . you'll be at home When you have found How very good the roving life is! For one's home, all the world, and for law each goes his way! Best of all, like wine to the senses: The life that's free! The life that's free!	Ah! Le mot n'est pas galant, Mais, qu'importe! Va . . . tu t'y feras Quand tu verras Comme c'est beau, la vie errante, Pour pays l'univers; et pour loi, ta volonté! Et surtout, la chose enivrante: La liberté! La liberté!

ALL
(to Don José)

We'll take you where no-one will find you, There with Carmen riding behind you; With us, you'll soon be at home	Suis nous à travers la campagne, Viens avec nous dans la montagne, Suis nous, et tout t'y feras

† Bizet altered the direction on this line from *'changing his tone and talking to Don José'* to *'toujours gaiment'*.

When you have found, up there,
How very good the roving life is,
For one's home, all the world, and for law
each goes his way!
Best of all, like wine to the senses,
The life that's free! The life that's free!

Quand tu verras, là-bas,
Comme c'est beau, la vie errante,
Pour pays, l'univers; et pour loi, sa volonté!

Et surtout, la chose enivrante:
La liberté! La liberté!

Curtain.

The brilliant Spanish contralto, Maria Gay, and her husband, Giovanni Zenatello, as Carmen and Don José.

Act Three

Entr'acte. [25]

The curtain rises on rocks ... A picturesque and wild spot ... completely deserted. Dark night. After a few moments, a smuggler appears above on the rocks, then another, and another. Smugglers appear here and there, climbing down the rocks. The men are carrying large bales on their shoulders.

Scene One. *Carmen, José, Dancairo, Remendado, Frasquita, Mercedes, Smugglers. / No. 18 Introduction, Sextet and Chorus*

[26]

CHORUS
(very quietly)

Be careful, be careful do not let them hear you, Fortune's waiting, waiting down below, One mistake now, and we are done for, And so be careful how you go!	Écoute, compagnon, écoute, La fortune est là-bas, là-bas, Mais prends garde pendant la route, Prends garde de faire un faux pas!

DANCAIRO, JOSE, CARMEN, MERCEDES AND FRASQUITA

Our kind of life can bring a fair reward,
   To follow it you need to have
     The courage that will dare, though!
Danger is there, you'll find it all around,
   It's down below, it's up above,
   It's everywhere,who cares though!
On we go straight ahead, unafraid of the flood,
     Unafraid of the storm,
     Unafraid of the danger,
Unafraid of the soldier who's waiting below,
     And will challenge the stranger!
Unafraid we go on straight ahead!
	Notre métier, notre métier est bon,
	   Mais pour le faire il faut avoir,
	     Avoir une âme forte,
	Et le péril, le péril est en haut,
	   Il est en bas, il est en haut,
	   Il est partout, qu'importe?
	Nous allons en avant, sans souci du torrent,
	     Sans souci du torrent,
	     Sans souci de l'orage,
	Sans souci du soldat qui là-bas nous attend,
	
	     Et nous guette au passage.
	Sans souci nous allons en avant!

ALL

Be careful, be careful, do not let them hear you, Fortune's waiting, waiting down below. One mistake now and we are done for, And so be careful how you go!	Écoute, compagnon, écoute, La fortune est là-bas, là-bas ... Mais prends garde pendant la route, Prends garde de faire un faux pas!

DANCAIRO

We're going to stop here ... Those who are tired can sleep for half an hour ...	Halte! Nous allons nous arrêter ici ... ceux qui ont sommeil pourrant dormir pendant une demi-heure ...

REMENDADO
(stretching luxuriously)

Ah!	Ah!

DANCAIRO

I'm going to see how we can get our goods into the town ... there is a breach in the wall that we could get through, but [unfortunately] they've posted a guard [in front of it].	Je vais, moi, voir s'il y a un moyen de faire entrer les marchandises dans la ville ... une brèche s'est faite dans le mur d'enceinte et nous pourrions passer par là; malheureusement on a mis un factionnaire pour garder cette brèche.

Lillas Pastia says [that] the guard tonight will be one of ours . . .	Lillas Pastia nous a fait savoir que, cette nuit, ce factionnaire serait un homme à nous . . .

DANCAIRO

Yes, but Lillas Pastia could be wrong . . . His guard might have been changed, so I'm going to make sure for myself, [before going any further] . . .	Oui, mais Lillas Pastia a pu se tromper . . . le factionnaire qu'il veut dire a pu être changé . . . Avant d'aller plus loin je ne trouve pas mauvais de m'assurer moi-même . . .
	(calling)
Remendado! . . .	Remendado! . . .

REMENDADO
(waking up)

Eh?	Hé?

DANCAIRO

Get up, you're coming with me . . .	Debout, tu vas venir avec moi . . .

REMENDADO

But, boss . . .	Mais, patron . . .

DANCAIRO

What was that?	Qu'est-ce que c'est?

REMENDADO
(getting up)

I'm coming, boss, I'm coming! . . .	Voilá, patron, voilá! . . .

DANCAIRO

[You go ahead.]	Allons, passe devant.

REMENDADO

And there was I, dreaming of a nice sleep!	Et moi qui rêvais que j'allais pouvoir dormir . . .
(going off followed by Dancairo)	
Only a dream! . . . Such a lovely dream!	C'était un rêve, hélas! c'était un rêve! . . .

Scene Two. *During the scene that follows, some of the gipsies light a fire, near which Mercedes and Frasquita come and sit; the rest roll themselves up in their cloaks, lie down and sleep. Carmen José. Frasquita, Mercedes, Smugglers.*

JOSE

Look, Carmen . . . if I was angry I'm sorry. Let's make peace . . .	Voyons, Carmen . . . si je t'ai parlé trop durement, je t'en demande pardon, faisons la paix.

CARMEN

No.	Non.

JOSE

Don't you love me any more?	Tu ne m'aimes plus, alors?

CARMEN

I only know I love you a lot less than I used to . . . [and if you go on like this, I shan't love you at all . . .] I won't be pestered and ordered about. I want to be free [to do as I please]!	Ce qui est sûr, c'est que je t'aimes beaucoup moins qu'autrefois . . . , et que si tu continues à t'y prendre de cette façon-là, je finirai par ne plus t'aimer du tout . . . Je ne veux pas être tourmentée ni surtout commandée. Ce que je veux, c'est être libre et faire ce qu'il me plaît.

JOSE

You're a devil, Carmen.	Tu es le diable, Carmen?

CARMEN

Yes.   Oui.

(Pause. He stares out over the landscape.)

What are you staring at?   Qu'est-ce que tu regardes là, à quoi penses-tu?

JOSE

[I'm thinking that] down there ... [about twenty miles from here, there's a village, and] in that village lives an old lady, who believes I'm still honest ...

Je me dis que là-bas ... à sept ou huit lieues d'ici tout au plus, il y a un village, et dans ce village une bonne vieille femme qui croit que je suis encore un honnête homme ...

CARMEN

An old lady?   Une bonne vieille femme?

JOSE

[Yes,] my mother.   Oui, ma mère.

CARMEN

[Your mother ... You know] you should go back to her. You're not cut out for life with us ... [dog and wolf don't mate for long.]

Ta mère ... Eh bien là, vrai, tu ne ferais pas mal d'aller la retrouver, car décidément tu n'est pas fait pour vivre avec nous ... chien et loup ne font pas longtemps bon ménage ...

JOSE

Carmen ...   Carmen ...

CARMEN

[And anyhow the trade's dangerous for those like you, who won't take cover when they hear shots ... A lot of our people have lost their skins that way; your turn will come.

Sans compter que le métier n'est pas sans péril pour ceux qui, comme toi, refusent de se cacher quand ils entendent des coups de fusils ... plusieurs des nôtres y ont laissé leur peau, ton tour viendra.

JOSE

And yours ...] if you go on talking of parting, [and if you don't behave to me as I wish you to behave ...]

Et le tien aussi ... si tu me parles encore de nous séparer et si tu ne te conduis pas avec moi comme je veux que tu te conduises ...

CARMEN

You'll kill me, perhaps? ...   Tu me tuerais, peut-être? ...

(José does not answer.)

You will ... I've often seen in the cards that we shall die together.

A la bonne heure ... j'ai vu plusieurs fois dans les cartes que nous devrions finir ensemble.

(clicking her castanets)

[Bah! What will be, will be ...]   Bah! arrive qui plante ...

JOSE

You're a devil, Carmen.   Tu es le diable, Carmen?

CARMEN

Yes, I've told you that before ...   Mais oui, je te l'ai déjà dit ...

She turns her back on José and goes to sit next to Mercedes and Frasquita. After a moment's indecision José moves away and stretches out on the rocks. During the last part of the scene Mercedes and Frasquita have spread out the cards in front of them. / No. 19 Trio

FRASQUITA
[27]

Shuffle!   Mêlons!

MERCEDES

Cut them!   Coupons!

Right! There we are!   Bien! C'est cela!

MERCEDES

Three cards in a row . . .   Trois cartes ici . . .

FRASQUITA

Four below.   Quatre là.

MERCEDES AND FRASQUITA

So there we are; now say, my   Et maintenant, parlez, mes belles,
  beauties,
Say what's to be, come tell us of the   De l'avenir, donnez-nous des nouvelles;
  future.
Say who you know will let us down!   Dites-nous qui nous trahira,
Say who you know will be our own!   Dites-nous qui nous aimera.
Reply, reply, reply, reply!   Parlez, parlez, parlez, parlez!

MERCEDES

There I see a lover who's bold,   Moi, je vois un jeune amoureux
He's young and we shan't have a   Qui m'aime on ne peut d'avantage.
  carriage.

FRASQUITA

Well, mine's very rich and he's old;   Le mien est très riche et très vieux;
All the same, he's talking of marriage!   Mais il parle de mariage.

MERCEDES
(proudly)

I am riding there on his horse   Je me campe sur son cheval,
And off to the hills he will sweep me!   Et dans la montagne il m'entraîne.

FRASQUITA

I live in a castle of course,   Dans un château presque royal,
And there like a queen he will keep   Le mien m'installe en souveraine.
  me!

MERCEDES

I'll have love, and love without end,   De l'amour à n'en plus finir,
Every day a riot of pleasure!   Tous les jours nouvelles folies.

FRASQUITA
(joyfully)

More gold than I know how to spend,   De l'or tant que j'en puis tenir,
Jewellery, pearls, diamonds, treasure!   Des diamants . . . des pierreries.

MERCEDES

My lover is soon made a chief,   Le mien devient un chef fameux,
He's followed by hundreds of fine   Cent hommes marchent à sa suite.
  men!

FRASQUITA

And mine . . . and mine . . . oh! it's   Le mien, en croirai-je mes yeux . . .
  past all belief . . .
(wildly)
Yes he dies! Ah! All his wealth will   Oui! Il meurt! Ah, je suis veuve et
  be mine then!   j'hérite.

BOTH

Come say once more, now say my   Parlez encore, parlez, mes belles,
  beauties,
Say what's to be. Come tell us of the   De l'avenir, donnez-nous des nouvelles;
  future.
Say who you know will let us down!   Dites-nous qui nous trahira.
Say who you know will be our own!   Dites-nous qui nous aimera.

(They start to look at the cards again.)

FRASQUITA

A fortune!	Fortune!

MERCEDES

Mine's love!	Amour!

CARMEN
(who is watching Mercedes and Frasquita play)

Let's see — it is my turn to try.	Voyons, que j'essaie à mon tour.

(She begins to turn up the cards.)

Diamond! Spade! It's death!	Carreau, pique ... la mort!
I can see ... I'm the first.	J'ai bien lu ... moi d'abord.

(pointing to the sleeping Don José)

Then I see him ... there for us both, it's death!	Ensuite lui ... pour tous les deux la mort!

(in a low voice, shuffling the cards)

You never can escape their unrelenting answer,	[28] En vain pour éviter les réponses amères,
However hard you try!	En vain tu mêleras,
You only waste your time, because the cards are honest	Cela ne sert à rien, les cartes sont sincères
And will not tell a lie!	Et ne mentiront pas!
If in the book of fate your happiness is written,	Dans le livre d'en haut, si ta page est heureuse,
Then deal and have no fear,	Mêle et coupe sans peur,
For every card you turn, to look into your future,	La carte sous tes doigts se tournera joyeuse
Will show good fortune there.	T'annonçant le bonheur!
But if you are to die, the terrifying sentence	Mais si tu dois mourir, si le mot redoutable
Is written there on high,	Est écrit par le sort,
Though you deal twenty times ... the cards will show no mercy —	Recommence vingt fois ... la carte impitoyable
They still repeat: "You die!"	Répètera: la mort!

(turning the cards again)

And there ... and there ... each time: "You die!"	Encore! encore! Toujours la mort!

FRASQUITA, MERCEDES

Come say once more, now say my beauties,	Parlez encore, parlez, mes belles,
Say what's to be, come tell us of the future;	De l'avenir, donnez-nous des nouvelles;
Say who you know will let us down!	Dites-nous qui nous trahira.
Say who you know will be our own!	Dites-nous qui nous aimera.
Reply, reply!	Parlez encore!

CARMEN †

You die! You die! There's no escape!	Encore! Encore! le désespoir!
You die! You die! Again you die!	La mort! La mort! Encore la mort!
Each time: you die! Again! Again!	Toujours: la mort. Encore! Encore!*

(Re-enter Dancairo and Remendado.)

Scene Three. *Carmen, José, Frasquita, Mercedes, Dancairo, Remendado.*

CARMEN

Well? ...	Eh bien? ...

DANCAIRO

I was right not to rely on Lillas Pastia; [we didn't find his man, but on the contrary]	Eh bien, j'avais raison de ne pas me fier aux renseignements de Lillas Pastia; nous

---

† Bizet inserted these exclamations, but cut a final couplet:
   Bah! qu'importe après tout, qu'importe? ...
   Carmen bravera tout, Carmen est la plus forte!

* Following the 1875 vocal score, it would be correct to spell 'encore' without the final 'e' but the usual spelling has been adopted here for consistency.

we found three customs men guarding the breach — guarding it very well ...

n'avons pas trouvé son factionnaire, mais en revanche nous avons aperçu trois douaniers qui gardaient la brèche et qui la gardaient bien, je vous assure ...

CARMEN

Do you know their names?

Savez-vous leurs noms à ces douaniers?

REMENDADO

Of course we know their names; [if *we* didn't know them, who on earth would?] There was Eusebéo, Perez and Bartolomé.

Certainement nous savons leurs noms; qui est-ce qui connaîtrait les douaniers si nous ne les connaissions pas? Il y avait Eusebio, Perez et Bartolomé.

FRASQUITA

Eusébeo ...

Eusebio ...

MERCEDES

Perez ...

Perez ...

CARMEN

And Bartolomé ...

Et Bartolomé ...

(laughing)

Don't worry, Dancairo, *we'll* look after your three guards!

N'ayez pas peur, Dancaîre, nous vous en répondons de vos trois douaniers ...

JOSE
(furious)

Carmen! ...

Carmen! ...

DANCAIRO

[We've had just about enough of you and your jealousy] ... No time to waste ... It's almost daylight ... Let's go.

Ah! toi tu vas nous laisser tranquilles avec ta jalousie ... le jour vient et nous n'avons pas de temps à perdre ... En route, les enfants.

(They take up their bales. Turning to José:)

*[As for you, you can guard the merchandise we're not taking with us ... Position yourself on that hill ... it'll be a marvellous vantage point, and if you see somebody following us I give you full permission to vent your temper on him.] — Are we ready?

Quant à toi, je te confie la garde des marchandises que nous n'emporterons pas ... Tu vas te placer là, sur cette hauteur ... tu y seras à merveille pour voir si nous sommes suivis ... dans le cas où tu apercevrais quelqu'un, je t'autorise à passer ta colère sur l'indiscret. — Nous y sommes?

REMENDADO

Yes, boss.

Oui, patron.

DANCAIRO

Then let's go ...

En route alors ...

(to the women)

You're not kidding yourselves; you are *sure* about the three guards?

Mais vous ne vous flattez pas, vous ne répondez vraiment de ces trois douaniers?

CARMEN

Don't *worry*, Dancairo.

N'ayez pas peur, Dancaîre.

No. 20 Ensemble

CARMEN, FRASQUITA, MERCEDES

Leave our three guards for us to deal with!
They're only human and love to please,
With ladies they love to be gallant;
So you let us go on in front!

[29] Quant au douanier, c'est notre affaire!
Tout comme un autre il aime à plaire,
Il aime à faire le galant,
Ah! laissez-nous passer en avant!

---

* *Alternative:* You stand guard over there and if you see someone following us, you can work off your temper on him.

CARMEN, MERCEDES, FRASQUITA AND THE WOMEN

Leave our three guards for us to deal with!
So you let us go on in front!

Quant au douanier c'est notre affaire,

Laissez-nous passer en avant.

CARMEN

My young guard will be so blind!

Et le douanier sera charmant.

MERCEDES

My young guard will be so fond!

Le douanier sera galant.

FRASQUITA

Oh yes, the guard will do anything we want!

Oui, le douanier sera même entreprenant!

ALL THREE WOMEN AND THE MEN

Leave our three guards for them/us to deal with!
They're only human and love to please!
With ladies, they love to be gallant,
So you let us go on in front!

Oui, le douanier, c'est leur/notre affaire!
Tout comme un autre il aime à plaire,
Il aime à faire le galant,
Laissez-nous passer en avant.

CARMEN, FRASQUITA, MERCEDES

No need to fight if we are clever;
It only means having his arm
Around our waist – getting together
While he enjoys using his charm.

Il ne s'agit plus de bataille,
Non, il s'agit tout simplement
De se laisser prendre la taille
Et d'écouter un compliment.

If it's a smile that he is after,
Oh well, why not: he'll have that too!

S'il faut aller jusqu'au sourire,
Que voulez-vous? on sourira!

CARMEN, FRASQUITA, MERCEDES AND THE WOMEN

And already we can assure you,
Our contraband all will get through.

Et d'avance, je puis le dire,
La contrebande passera.

CARMEN, FRASQUITA, MERCEDES AND FULL CHORUS

Come along! Get on! Come along!
Leave our three guards for us to deal with!
　(etc.)

En avant! Marchons, allons, en avant!
Quant au douanier c'est notre affaire,
　(etc.)

All the smugglers go off. José brings up the rear, examining the priming pin of his gun; just before he goes off a man looks out from behind a rock. It is a guide. He enters stealthily, then signals to Micaela, who is still off-stage.

Scene Four. *The Guide, then Micaela.*

GUIDE

Here we are.

Nous y sommes.

MICAELA
(*entering*)

[Is this it?

C'est ici.

GUIDE

Yes, a horrible place, isn't it, enough to send shivers up your spine!

Oui, vilain endroit, n'est-ce pas, et pas rassurant du tout?

MICAELA

I can't see anyone.

Je ne vois personne.

GUIDE

They've just left, but they'll be back again soon, as they haven't taken all their merchandise . . . I know their habits . . . Be careful . . . there's generally a guard on here, and if he saw us . . .

Ils viennent de partir, mais ils reviendront bientôt, car ils n'ont pas emporté toutes leurs marchandises . . . je connais leurs habitudes . . . prenez garde . . . l'un des leurs doit être en sentinelle quelque part et si l'on nous apercevait . . .

MICAELA

I hope someone will see me . . . since the reason I came here was to speak to . . . was to speak to one of these smugglers . . .]

J'espère bien qu'on m'apercevra . . . puisque je suis venue ici tout justement pour parler à . . . pour parler à un de ces contrabandiers . . .

GUIDE

You've certainly got courage . . . [Just now, when we got caught up in that herd of wild bulls being driven by the famous Escamillo, you didn't turn a hair . . . And now you're] coming up here to face these gipsies . . .

Eh bien là, vrai, vous pouvez vous vanter d'avoir du courage . . . Tout à l'heure quand nous nous sommes trouvés au milieu de ce troupeau de taureaux sauvages qui conduisait le célèbre Escamillo, vous n'avez pas tremblé . . . Et maintenant venir ainsi affronter ces Bohémiens . . .

MICAELA

I'm not easily scared.

Je ne suis pas facile à effrayer.

GUIDE

[You're only saying that because I'm here with you . . . but if you were alone . . .

Vous dites cela parce que je suis près de vous, mais si vous étiez toute seule . . .

MICAELA

I shan't be frightened, I promise.

Je n'aurais pas peur, je vous assure.

GUIDE

You're sure? . . .

Bien vrai? . . .

MICAELA

Quite sure . . .

Bien vrai . . .

GUIDE
(*naively*)

Well in that case I'd like to go back — I agreed to act as your guide because you paid me well; but now you're here . . . if you don't mind I'll wait for you below . . . at the inn where you found me.

Alors je vous demanderai la permission de m'en aller. — J'ai consenti à vous servir de guide parce que vous m'avez bien payé; mais maintenant que vous êtes arrivée . . . si ça ne vous fait rien, j'irai vous attendre là, où vous m'avez pris . . . à l'auberge qui est au bas de la montagne.

MICAELA

Alright, wait for me there!

C'est cela, allez m'attendre!

GUIDE

You're sure you want to stay?

Vous restez décidément?

MICAELA

Yes, I'm staying!] *

Oui, je reste!

GUIDE

May [all] the saints protect you . . . [you've some odd ideas . . .]

Que tous les saints de paradis vous soient en aide alors, mais c'est une drôle d'idée que vous avez là . . .
(*Exit.*)

Scene Five. / *No. 21 Aria.*

MICAELA
(*looking around her*)

[He was right . . . it's a horrible place!]

Mon guide avait raison . . . l'endroit n'est pas bien rassurant . . .

---

* Alternative: GUIDE: I'm going back to the inn, I'll wait for you there.

I said there was nothing could scare [30] me, I said I'd stay here all alone tonight; But though I try to act so bravely, Yet in my heart I die of fright! Here on this dreadful mountain I'm alone and afraid, but wrong to be afraid! You'll give me courage and protection, For you are by my side, O Lord!	Je dis que rien ne m'épouvante, Je dis, hélas! que je réponds de moi: Mais j'ai beau faire la vaillante, Au fond du cœur, je meurs d'effroi ... Seule, en ce lieu sauvage Toute seule j'ai peur, mais j'ai tort d'avoir peur; Vous me donnerez du courage, Vous me protégerez, Seigneur!

I shall meet that creature at last [31] Whose wicked cunning I can see, Led astray to crime and dishonour That man who means the world to me! A dangerous women and a beauty! Yet I will never be afraid! I'll tell her the truth when I face her, Ah! For you are there protecting me ...	Je vais voir de près cette femme Dont les artifices maudits Ont fini par faire un infâme De celui que j'aimais jadis! Elle est dangereuse, elle est belle! Mais je ne veux pas avoir peur! Je parlerai haut devant elle, Ah! Seigneur, vous me protégerez,

Watch over me, O Lord! †	Protégez-moi, Seigneur.

MICAELA

Heavens ... I'm certain ... a hundred paces away ... on that rock ... I'm sure that's Don José—	Mais ... je ne me trompe pas ... à cent pas d'ici ... sur ce rocher ... c'est Don José —

(calling)

José, José! —	José, José! ...

(frightened)

But what's he doing ... He's not looking in my direction ... He's raising his gun ... he's taking aim ... he's going to shoot.	Mais que fait-il? ... Il ne regarde pas de mon côté ... il arme sa carabine, il ajuste ... il fait feu ...

(A gunshot is heard.)

Oh I've trusted my courage too much ... I'm frightened ... I'm frightened.	Ah! mon Dieu, j'ai trop presumé de mon courage ... J'ai peur! ... J'ai peur!

She disappears behind the bales. At the same time Escamillo enters holding his hat in his hand.

Scene Six. *Escamillo, then Don José.*

ESCAMILLO
(looking at his hat)

A fraction lower ... and it wouldn't have been *me* who'd have had the pleasure of fighting the bulls we've been rounding up ...	Quelques lignes plus bas ... et ce n'est pas moi qui, à la course prochaine, aurais eu le plaisir de combattre les taureaux que je suis en train de conduire ...

(Enter Don José.)

JOSE
(his knife in his hand)

Who are you? Answer!	Qui êtes-vous? Répondez!

ESCAMILLO
(very calmly)

Hey there! Go easy!	Eh là ... doucement!

No. 22 Duet

ESCAMILLO

My name is Escamillo, toreador of Granada.	Je suis Escamillo, torrero de Grenade.

---

† Bizet cut and repeated the first verse, instead of using the third verse text supplied.

Escamillo! Escamillo!

ESCAMILLO

That's me. C'est moi.

JOSE
(putting his knife back in his belt)

I have heard of your fame. Je connais votre nom,
You're very welcome here; but really one Soyez le bienvenu; mais vraiment,
step further camarade,
And you'd have stayed for good! Vous pouviez y rester.

ESCAMILLO

My impression was the same. Je ne vous dis pas non.
But you see I'm in love my friend, yes, Mais je suis amoureux, mon cher, à la folie,
quite insanely!
And surely he would prove unworthy of Et celui-là serait un pauvre compagnon
his flame,
Who would not risk his life to go and see Qui, pour voir ses amours, ne risquerait
his lady! sa vie!

JOSE

Then you're coming to find her up here? Celle que vous aimez est ici?

ESCAMILLO

That's the game — Justement.
A lovely gipsy girl, my friend. C'est une zingara, mon cher.

JOSE

What is her name? Elle s'appelle?

ESCAMILLO

Carmen. Carmen.

JOSE
(aside)

Carmen! Carmen!

ESCAMILLO

Carmen, yes my friend. Her lover used to Carmen, oui mon cher. Elle avait pour
be amant
A soldier who for love of her had turned Un soldat qui jadis a déserté pour elle.
deserter.

JOSE
(aside)

Carmen! Carmen!

ESCAMILLO

Oh how they loved! It's over now I Ils s'adoraient. Mais c'est fini, je crois,
hear,
Love affairs with Carmen last barely half Les amours de Carmen ne durent pas six
a year. mois.

JOSE

Yet you love her, you say . . . Vous l'aimez cependant . . .

ESCAMILLO

I love her. Je l'aime.
Yes, my friend, adore her, adore her quite Oui, mon cher, je l'aime, je l'aime à la folie!
insanely.

JOSE

But if stealing our gipsy girls is what Mais pour nous enlever nos filles de
you're after, Bohême,
You understand you have to pay? . . . Savez-vous bien qu'il faut payer? . . .

ESCAMILLO
(cheerfully)

Right! Then I'll pay.   Soit, on paiera.

JOSE
(threateningly)

The price you have to pay is paid with a   Et que le prix se paie à coups de navaja!
dagger!

ESCAMILLO
(surprised)

Is paid with a dagger?   A coups de navaja?

JOSE

You understand?   Comprenez-vous?

ESCAMILLO
(ironically)

The idea's very clear!   Le discours est très net.
This ex-Dragoon, this soldier that she   Ce déserteur, ce beau soldat qu'elle
loves so,   aime,
Or rather, used to love, must be you?   Ou du moins qu'elle aimait, c'est donc
                                            vous?

JOSE

Yes, I'm the soldier!   Oui, c'est moi-même.

ESCAMILLO

Delighted, my dear friend! So I take your   J'en suis ravi, mon cher, et le tour est
place with her.   complet.

Daggers drawn, each wraps his cloak round his arm.

JOSE

At last all my anger   Enfin ma colère
Finds a target now, and blood,   Trouve à qui parler.
His blood will start to flow,   Le sang, je l'espère,
I hope, will start to flow.   Va bientôt couler!

ESCAMILLO

Well that was a blunder,   Quelle maladresse!
How it makes me laugh!   J'en rirais vraiment!
To look for one's mistress   Chercher la maîtresse
And find her former lover!   Et trouver l'amant!

BOTH

You be on your guard!   Mettez-vous en garde
And defend yourself!   Et veillez sur vous!
Too bad if you're slow   Tant pis pour qui tarde
To avoid the knife!   A parer les coups!

They take up their positions on guard some distance apart.

ESCAMILLO

I know the guard you use, the Navarraise;   Je la connais, ta garde navarraise,
That, I warn you now as a friend,   Et je te préviens en ami,
Won't be any help ...   Qu'elle ne vaut rien ...

Don José, without replying, sets upon the Torero.

Take it easy!   A ton aise.
I wanted to be sure you were warned.   Je t'aurai du moins averti.

They fight. The Torero, very calm, merely defends himself.

JOSE
(furious)

You're not fighting, you cheat.   Tu m'épargnes, maudit.

113

ESCAMILLO

At any game of knives,	A ce jeu de couteau
I'm far too sharp for you.	Je suis trop fort pour toi.

JOSE

That we shall see!	Voyons cela.

A very fast and lively hand-to-hand fight. Don José is at the mercy of the Torero who does not strike him.

ESCAMILLO

There you are!	Tout beau!
(with dignity)	
Your life rests with me, but the truth is	Ta vie est à moi, mais en somme
My proper trade is to strike down the bull,	J'ai pour métier de frapper le taureau,
And not to butcher fellow humans!	Non de trouer le cœur de l'homme.

JOSE

Fight now or you die! You won't find this a game.	Frappe ou bien meurs . . . Ceci n'est pas un jeu.

ESCAMILLO
(releasing him)

Right! But at least, do take your time!	Soit, mais au moins respire un peu.

JOSE, ESCAMILLO

You be on your guard	Mettez vous en garde
(etc.)	*(etc.)*

They start fighting again. Escamillo slips and falls on the grass (or, as in the 1875 vocal score, his knife breaks)*. Don José is about to strike him. Carmen and Dancairo rush in.

CARMEN
(grabbing Don José's arm)

Hola, José! . . .	Hola, José! . . .

The Torero gets up; Remendado, Mercedes, Frasquita and the smugglers have come back.

ESCAMILLO
(getting up)

Ah! What pleasure it gives me	Vrai, j'ai l'âme ravie
That it was you, Carmen, who came in time to save me.	Que ce soit vous, Carmen, qui me sauviez la vie.

CARMEN

Escamillo!	Escamillo!

ESCAMILLO
(to Don José, cheerfully condescending)

As for you, soldier boy,	Quant à toi, beau soldat,
The game's not yet decided, we'll fight to win the lady:	Nous sommes manche à manche et nous jouerons la belle,
So when you want to try again, you name the day.	Le jour ou tu voudras reprendre le combat.

DANCAIRO
(intervening)

Alright! Alright! Leave it till later,	C'est bon, c'est bon, plus de querelle!
Come, for we must be off.	Nous, nous allons partir.
(to Escamillo)	
And you, my friend, goodnight!	Et toi, l'ami, bonsoir.

ESCAMILLO

Before I go, at least you'll concede me the right	Souffrez au moins qu'avant de vous dire au revoir,

---

* See Winton Dean p. 24

To invite you, one and all, to see me in Sevilla,	Je vous invite tous aux courses de Séville.
For there I am intending to shine at the fight,	Je compte pour ma part y briller de mon mieux,

(looking at Carmen)

Those who love me will come.	Et qui m'aime y viendra.

(coldly to Don José who made a threatening gesture)

My friend, don't get excited!	L'ami, tiens-toi tranquille,

(to Carmen)

That is all, all I've to say, yes I've no more to do except bid you goodnight.	J'ai tout dit, oui j'ai tout dit, et je n'ai plus ici qu'à faire mes adieux . . .

[17]

Don José turns to attack Escamillo but Dancairo and Remendado hold him back. Escamillo goes off very slowly. Carmen follows him with her eyes.

JOSE
(to Carmen, with a suppressed threat)

Better take care, Carmen, I won't stand any more . . .	Prends garde à toi, Carmen . . . je suis las de souffrir . . .

Carmen replies to Don José with a shrug of her shoulders and moves away.

DANCAIRO

We're starting, we're starting . . . it's time to go . . .	En route . . . en route . . . il faut partir . . .

ALL

We're starting, we're starting . . . it's time to go . . .	En route . . . en route . . . il faut partir . . .

REMENDADO

Stop! Look, there is someone there, trying to hide!	Halte! . . . Quelqu'un est là qui cherche à se cacher.

He leads Micaela out of hiding.

CARMEN

It's a girl, too!	Une femme!

DANCAIRO

Good Lord! An unusual pleasure!	Pardieu, la surprise est heureuse.

JOSE
(recognising Micaela)

Micaela! . . .	Micaela! . . .

MICAELA

Don José! . . .	Don José! . . .

JOSE

You're in danger! Whatever brings you here?	Malheureuse! Que viens-tu faire ici?

MICAELA

Me? I came here for you . . .	Moi, je viens te chercher . . .
Down there, nearly despairing, [11]	Là-bas est la chaumière
She is waiting at home,	Où, sans cesse priant,
All alone there your mother	Une mère, ta mère,
Prays in tears for you, her son!	Pleure, hélas! sur son enfant . . .
Through her tears she prays you'll hear her,	Elle pleure et t'appelle,
Calls and holds out her arms for you!	Elle pleure et te tend les bras.
Oh come home and be near her,	Tu prendras pitié d'elle,
José come home to her, oh do!	José, tu me suivras.

CARMEN
(to Don José, hammering it out)

Go on, go on, it's better so,	Va-t'en! Va-t'en! Tu feras bien,
Our sort of life's no good to you.	Notre métier ne te vaut rien.

JOSE
(to Carmen)

Do you tell me to go then?	Tu me dis de la suivre?

CARMEN

Yes, you should go today.	Oui, tu devrais partir.

JOSE

So that you can then run away	Pour que toi tu puisses courir
To that other man you want.	Après ton nouvel amant.
No! No: I won't —	Non, non vraiment,

(resolutely)

For me death before I leave you!	[32] Dût-il m'en coûter la vie,
No, Carmen, I'll never go, not I!	Non, Carmen, je ne partirai pas!
For our lives are bound together,	Et la chaîne qui nous lie
Bound together, till we die!	Nous liera jusqu'au trépas . . .

MICAELA

Don José, it's your mother	Écoute-moi, je t'en prie,
Who entreats you not to stay,	Ta mère te tend les bras,
And what binds your lives together,	Cette chaîne qui te lie,
José, you must break today!	José, tu la briseras.

CHORUS

It is death unless you leave her.	Il t'en coûtera la vie,
José! You must go away,	José, si tu ne pars pas,
And what binds your lives together,	Et la chaîne qui vous lie
You must break or you will die.	Se rompra par ton trépas.

MICAELA

Oh please! Don José!	Hélas! Don José!

JOSE
(to Micaela)

Let me be! For I know I am damned!	Laissez-moi, car je suis condamné!

JOSE
(to Carmen)

You are mine, daughter of Satan!	Je te tiens, fille damnée,
I will make you yield again	Et je te forcerai bien
To the destiny that made us	A subir la destinée
That welded your fate to mine!	Qui rive ton sort au mien.
For me death before I leave you,	Dût-il m'en couter la vie,
No, Carmen, I'll never go, not I!	Non, Carmen, je ne partirai pas!

FRASQUITA, MERCEDES, REMENDADO, DANCAIRO AND CHORUS

Ah! Be careful! Be careful, Don José!	Ah! prends garde, prends garde, Don José!

MICAELA
(with authority)

I've one more word to say and I won't speak again.	Une parole encore!. . . ce sera la dernière.
Your mother is ill! She's ill and she's dying!	Hélas, José, ta mère se meurt . . . et ta mere
And your mother would never want to die without pardoning you!	Ne voudrait pas mourir sans t'avoir pardonné!

JOSE

My mother!. . . Going to die . . .	Ma mère . . . elle se meurt . . .

MICAELA

Yes, Don José!	Oui, don José.

JOSE

Let's go! Ah! Let's go! . . .	Partons . . . Ah! partons!
(to Carmen)	
Rest assured . . . I'm going, but we'll meet again!	Sois contente, je pars, mais nous nous reverrons.

[3a]
(He leads Micaela off.)

ESCAMILLO
(off-stage from far away)

Toreador, on guard now!	Toreador, en garde,
Toreador! Toreador!	Toreador! Toreador!
Do not forget that, when you draw your sword,	Et songe en combattant
Two dark eyes look down,	Qu'un œil noir te regarde
And love is your reward.	Et que l'amour t'attend.

[17]

Hearing Escamillo's voice, José stops upstage among the rocks . . . watching Carmen, who is listening; he hesitates a moment . . .

JOSE

Micaela, let's go.	Micaela, partons.

Don José and Micaela disappear. Carmen leans, listening, on the rocks. The gipsies have taken up their bales and start off.*

CARMEN: C'était écrit! Cela doit être: Moi d'abord . . . et puis lui . . . Le destin est le maître.
* This text originally in the libretto was not set to music. The end of the act involved a partial repeat of the ensemble.

Miguel Fléta as Don José (Stuart-Liff Collection)

Act Four

A square in Seville. At the back of the stage, the walls of the old arenas. The entrance to the bullring is closed by a long canvas curtain. It is the day of the bull-fight. The square is very busy. Water-sellers, orange-sellers, fan-sellers etc..

Scene One. *Zuniga, Andres, Frasquita, Mercedes, Carmen, Escamillo. / No. 24 Chorus.*

CHORUS OF SELLERS

Two pesetas!	A deux cuartos,
Two pesetas!	A deux cuartos,
Fans here for you to fan yourselves!	Des éventails pour s'éventer,
Oranges to refresh yourselves!	Des oranges pour grignoter,
Buy a programme! Read all the names!	Le programme avec les détails
Good wine! Water! Best cigarettes!	Du vin, de l'eau, des cigarettes
Two pesetas!	A deux cuartos,
Two pesetas!	A deux cuartos,
All at two pesetas,	Voyez! à deux cuartos!
Señoras and Caballeros!	Señoras et caballeros ...

During the first chorus, Zuniga and Andres, with Frasquita and Mercedes on their arms, have entered.

ZUNIGA

Bring some oranges, quickly ...   Des oranges, vite ...

VARIOUS ORANGE SELLERS
(hurrying up)

Here you are —   En voici ...
Please take your choice now Señnorita.   Prenez, prenez, mesdemoiselles.

ORANGE SELLER
(to Zuniga, who is paying her)

You're kind, my good Señor, many   Merci, mon officier, merci.
  thanks!

OTHER ORANGE SELLERS

Look at these, Señor, they're much   Celles-ci, señor, sont plus belles ...
  sweeter!

FAN SELLERS

Fans here for you to fan yourselves!   Des éventails pour s'éventer!

ORANGE SELLERS

Oranges to refresh yourselves!   Des oranges pour grignoter!

PROGRAMME SELLER

Buy a programme, read all the names!   Le programme avec les détails.

WINE SELLERS

Good wine!   Du vin ...

WATER SELLERS

Watér!   De l'eau.

CIGARETTE SELLERS

Best cigarettes!   Des cigarettes.

ANDRES

Hey you! I want a fan!   Holà! des éventails.

GIPSY
(hurrying up to Andres)

Would señor be needing some glasses?   Voulez-vous aussi des lorgnettes?

118

Two pesetas!	A deux cuartos,
Two pesetas!	A deux cuartos,
All at two pesetas,	Voyez à deux cuartos,
Señoras and Caballeros!	Señoras et caballeros.
Two pesetas	A deux cuartos,
Two pesetas	A deux cuartos,
Buy some today!	Voyez, voyez.

ZUNIGA

What have you done with Carmencita?	Qu'avez-vous donc fait de la Carmencita?
[I can't see her anywhere.]	je ne la vois pas.

FRASQUITA

[She'll be here in a moment . . .] Escamillo's here, so Carmen won't be far away.	Nous la verrons tout à l'heure . . . Escamillo est ici, la Carmencita ne doit pas être loin.

ANDRES

Ah! It's Escamillo now?	Ah! c'est Escamillo maintenant?

MERCEDES

[She's mad about him . . .]	Elle en est folle . . .

FRASQUITA

And her old love José, what has happened to him?	Et son ancien amoureux José, sait-on ce qu'il est devenu? . . .

ZUNIGA

He turned up in the village where his mother lived . . . But when the soldiers arrived to arrest him, he wasn't there . . .	Il a reparu dans le village où sa mère habitait . . . l'ordre avait même été donné de l'arrêter, mais quand les soldats sont arrivés, José n'était plus là . . .

MERCEDES

So now he's free?	En sorte qu'il est libre?

ZUNIGA

Yes, for the moment.	Oui, pour le moment.

FRASQUITA

Hum! I wouldn't be happy in Carmen's shoes . . . I wouldn't be happy at all!	Hum! je ne serais pas tranquille à la place de Carmen, je ne serais pas tranquille du tout.

Shouts off-stage . . . fanfares, etc.. It is the arrival of the Cuadrilla. / No. 25 Chorus and Scene. [1, 2]

URCHINS
(*off-stage*)

Here they are, here they are, here they are!	Les voici, les voici, les voici!

URCHINS (*entering*) AND CHORUS

Here they are, here come the Cuadrilla,	Les voici, voici la quadrille,
The Cuadrill' of the Toreros!	La quadrille des toreros,
How the lances shine in the sunlight!	Sur les lances le soleil brille,
Now up, up go your sombreros!	En l'air toques et sombreros!
Here they are, here come the Cuadrilla,	Les voici, voici la quadrille,
The Cuadrill' of the Toreros!	La quadrille des toreros.
Here they are, here they are, here they are!	Les voici, les voici, les voici!

(*Procession of the Cuadrilla. The Policemen — the Alguazils – enter.*)

Marching in and ready to chase us,	Voici, débouchant sur la place,
Here they come to push us about,	Voici d'abord, marchant au pas,

Policemen with their ugly faces.	L'alguazil à vilaine face,
Get out! Get out! Get out! Get out!	A bas! à bas! à bas! à bas!
Down with the police! Get out!	A bas l'Alguazil! à bas!

(*The Chulos and Banderilleros enter.*)

As they're marching by let us cheer them.	Et puis saluons au passage,
Give a cheer for the brave Chulos!	Saluons les hardis chulos,
Bravo! Bravo! How we admire them!	Bravo! viva! gloire au courage!
There they go, the brave Chulos!	Voici les hardis chulos!
Look there the Banderilleros,	Voyez les banderilleros!
And oh! how arrogant their bearing!	Voyez quel air de crânerie,
What haughty looks! And how the sun picks out	Voyez, quel regards! et de quel éclat
The gold-embroidered silk they're wearing	Étincelle la broderie
Upon their costumes for the fight!	De leur costume de combat.
There go the Banderilleros!	Voici les Banderilleros!

(*The Picadors enter.*)

And here is another Cuadrilla.	Une autre quadrille s'avance,
Look there, the Picadors! Ah! They look so grand!	Voyez les picadors comme ils sont beaux!
They will goad the bull with their lances	Comme ils vont du fer de leur lance
Till the blood is staining the sand!	Harceler le flanc des taureaux.
The Torero! The Torero! [17]	L'Espada! L'Espada!
Escamillo! Escamillo!	Escamillo! Escamillo!

(*Escamillo finally appears and with him Carmen, radiant and stunningly dressed.*)

Escamillo, blade of Granada,	C'est l'Espada, la fine lame,
Toreador, best of them all	Celui qui vient terminer tout,
He's the one who will end the drama,	Qui paraît à la fin du drame
He will strike and the bull will fall!	Et qui frappe le dernier coup.
Our Escamillo! Our Escamillo!	Vive, Escamillo! Vive, Escamillo!
Ah, bravo!	Ah, bravo!

ESCAMILLO
(*to Carmen*)

If you love me, Carmen, you will find, [34] very shortly	Si tu m'aimes, Carmen, tu pourras tout à l'heure
You can be proud of me.	Être fière de moi.

CARMEN

I love you, Escamillo, I love you, and may death take me,	Ah! je t'aime, Escamillo, je t'aime et que je meure,
If I have ever loved any man more than you!	Si j'ai jamais aimé quelqu'un autant que toi.

Sound of trumpets off-stage. Two trumpeters enter followed by four policemen.

POLICEMEN
(*off-stage*)

Way there!	Place,
Way there!	Place,
Way for His Worship the Mayor!	Place au Seigneur Alcade!

The crowd lines up to watch the mayor's procession.

URCHINS

His Worship! His Worship! His Worship!	L'alcade! L'alcade! L'alcade!

CHORUS

Don't be such a nuisance!	Pas de bousculade,
Let us take a look	Regardons passer
As he marches by,	Et se prélasser
At our worthy Lord Mayor!	Le Seigneur Alcade.

120

Way there! Way there! Way for His
Worship the Mayor!

Place, place au Seigneur Alcade!

The Mayor crosses the stage slowly, preceded and followed by policemen. Meanwhile, Frasquita and Mercedes go up to Carmen.

FRASQUITA

Carmen, take my advice, you'd better not
stay here.

Carmen, un bon conseil, ne reste pas ici.

CARMEN

And why not, may I ask?

Et pourquoi, s'il te plaît?

MERCEDES

He is here.

Il est là.

CARMEN

But who?

Qui donc?

MERCEDES

He!
Don José . . . Can't you see, in the crowd
there, he's hiding . . .

Lui,
Don José . . . dans la foule il se cache;
regarde.

CARMEN

Yes, I can see.

Oui, je le vois.

FRASQUITA

Be careful.

Prends garde.

CARMEN

I am not the sort to be frightened by him,
I have stayed as I've something to say.

Je ne suis pas femme à trembler devant lui.
Je l'attends . . . et je vais lui parler.

MERCEDES

Carmen, I'm right, be careful!

Carmen, crois moi, prends garde!

CARMEN

I'm not afraid!

Je ne crains rien!

FRASQUITA

Be careful!

Prends garde!

The mayor and the policemen enter the bullring. Behind the mayor's procession the Cuadrilla procession begins to move again into the bullring. The crowd follows . . . Don José is revealed. The orchestral theme [1] fades and dies away. On the last notes, Carmen and Don José are alone facing one another.

Scene Two. *Carmen, Don José. / No. 26 Duet, Finale.*

CARMEN
(*curtly*)

José.

C'est toi!

JOSE

Carmen!

C'est moi!

CARMEN

They came just now to warn me
That you were not far off, that you were
sure to stay;
And they told me my life itself might be in
danger;
But I am brave! And I shan't run away!

L'on m'avait avertie
Que tu n'étais pas loin, que tu devais venir;

L'on m'avait même dit de craindre pour
ma vie;
Mais je suis brave et n'ai pas voulu fuir.

I offer you no threat! I beg you, I implore you!
    All that has passed Carmen, is forgotten!
    Yes, we'll begin again,
    Start our life again together
    Far from here, away from Spain.

Je ne menace pas; j'implore, je supplie!
    Notre passé, Carmen, je l'oublie!
    Oui, nous allons tous deux
    Commencer une autre vie,
    Loin d'ici, sous d'autres cieux.

CARMEN

What you ask can never happen!
Carmen never yet has lied!
Her mind is made up completely,
For her and you . . . it's the end.
To you I've never lied . . .
For us both it's the end. .

Tu demandes l'impossible!
Carmen jamais n'a menti;
Son âme reste inflexible;
Entre elle et toi, tout est fini,
Jamais je n'ai menti;
Entre nous, tout est fini.

JOSE

Carmen, you've your life before you,
    O my Carmen, oh let me save you,
    Save you, for I adore you,
    Then you will have saved me too!

Carmen, il est temps encore,
    O ma Carmen, laisse-moi
    Te sauver, toi que j'adore,
    Et me sauver avec toi!

CARMEN

No, for I know it is time now,
And I know I'm going to die;
But if I live or if you kill me,
I'll not give in to you, not I.

Non, je sais bien que c'est l'heure,
Je sais bien que tu me tueras;
Mais que je vive ou que je meure,
Non, je ne te céderai pas!

JOSE

Ah! You've your life before you,
    O my Carmen, let me save you,
    Save you, for I adore you,
    Then you will have saved me too!

Carmen, il est temps encore,
    O ma Carmen laisse-moi
    Te sauver, toi que j'adore,
    Et me sauver avec toi!

CARMEN

But why waste your time adoring
Someone who's no longer free?
No use your saying: "I adore you!"
You will get no more from me.
    You waste your time,
    I'll give in no more,
    Not to you!

Pourquoi t'occuper encore
D'un cœur qui n'est plus à toi?
En vain tu dis: 'je t'adore!'
Tu n'obtiendras rien de moi.
    Ah! c'est en vain,
    Tu n'obtiendras rien,
    Rien de moi!

JOSE
(in anguish)

Then you don't love me at all?
(Carmen does not answer so Don José repeats, in despair:)
Then you don't love me at all!

Tu ne m'aimes donc plus?

Tu ne m'aimes donc plus!

CARMEN
(calmly)

No, I don't love you at all.

Non, je ne t'aime plus.

JOSE
(with passion)

But I still love you, more than ever, [35]
Carmen! I tell you I adore you!

Mais moi, Carmen, je t'aime encore;
Carmen, hélas! je t'adore.

CARMEN

Oh what's the good of that? A lot of useless words!

A quoi bon tout cela? que de mots superflus!

JOSE

Carmen, I tell you I adore you,
Alright, if that is what you want,

Carmen, je t'aime, je t'adore!
Eh bien, s'il le faut, pour te plaire,

I'll stay a bandit here, and I'll do all you ask . . .	Je resterai bandit, tout ce que tu voudras,
All! Do you hear, but don't desert me now, O my Carmen! Ah! Do recall, You must recall the past, how much in love we both were!	Tout, tu m'entends, mais ne me quitte pas, O ma Carmen, ah! souviens toi, Souviens-toi du passé, nous nous aimions naguère,

(desperately)

You cannot leave me now, Carmen! You cannot leave me now!	Ah! ne me quitte, Carmen, Ah! ne me quitte pas!

CARMEN

No, no! Carmen will not give way! Free she was born and free, free she will die.	Jamais Carmen ne cédera! Libre elle est née et libre elle mourra!

CHORUS
(from the bullring)

Bravo! What a fight to remember! [1, 2] Dripping blood on the sand See the bull they have goaded Returns back to the charge . . . Viva! Bravo! Oh Bravo! Oh bravo, Torero, oh bravo, Torero!	Viva! la course est belle, Sur le sable sanglant, Le taureau qu'on harcèle En bondissant s'élance . . . Viva! Bravo! Victoire! Voyez! Voyez! Victoire!

Both Carmen and José listen to the cheering in silence. Carmen, when she hears the final shouts herself lets out a cry of "Ah!" in pride and joy. Don José does not once take his eyes off her. As the chorus finishes Carmen moves towards the bullring.

JOSE
(barring her way)

Where are you going? . . .	Où vas-tu? . . .

CARMEN

Let me pass!	Laisse-moi.

JOSE

This fellow they are cheering, Is then your latest love!	Cet homme qu'on acclame, C'est ton nouvel amant!

CARMEN
(trying to get past)

Let me pass, let me pass!	Laisse-moi, laisse-moi!

JOSE

No, I swear it! I'll never let you pass, Carmen, I'll make you follow me!	Sur mon âme, Tu ne passeras pas, Carmen, c'est moi que tu suivras!

CARMEN

Let me pass, Don José, I'll never go with you.	Laisse-moi, don José! . . . Je ne te suivrai pas.

JOSE

You mean to go to him! Speak!	[3a] Tu va le retrouver . . . dis . . .

(with fury)

It's him you love?	Tu l'aimes donc?

CARMEN

I love him, I love him, and in face of death I repeat again that I love him.	Je l'aime, Je l'aime, et devant la mort même, Je répéterai que je l'aime.

CHORUS
(from the bullring)

Bravo, bravo! The bull is done for! Cut him clean to the heart! Down goes the toro! Bravo! Bravo, the Toreador! Bravo!	Viva! Bravo! Victoire! Frappé juste en plein cœur, Le taureau tombe! Gloire Gloire du torero vainqueur! Victoire!

JOSE
(violently)

And so, every hope of salvation	Ainsi, le salut de mon âme
Now I shall have lost all for you.	Je l'aurai perdu pour que toi,
For you to go running, you harlot,	Pour que tu t'en ailles, infâme!
Into his arms, laughing at me.	Entre ses bras, rire de moi.
No, by the saints, you'll not do that,	Non, par le sang, tu n'iras pas!
Carmen, for you're coming with me.	Carmen, c'est moi que tu suivras!

CARMEN

No! No! Never!	Non! non! jamais!

JOSE

I am tired of using threats!	Je suis las de te menacer!

CARMEN
(furiously)

All right, kill me at once, or let me go inside.	Eh bien! frappe-moi donc, ou laisse-moi passer.

CHORUS
(fanfares off-stage)

Escamillo!	Victoire!

JOSE
(out of his mind)

Now for the last time, you fiend,	Pour la dernière fois, démon,
Will you come with me?	Veux-tu me suivre?

CARMEN
(tearing a ring from her finger and throwing it hard at him)

No! No!	Non! non!
You remember this ring — the ring that	Cette bague, autrefois, tu me l'avais
once you gave me . . .	donnée . . .
Take it!	Tiens!

JOSE
(drawing his knife, moves in on Carmen)

For that, you die . . .	Eh bien, damnée . . .*

Carmen retreats . . . Don José pursues her . . . Fanfares and shouts in the arena.

CHORUS
(in the bullring)

Toreador on guard now!	[17]	Toreador, en garde,
Do not forget that when you draw your sword,		Et songe bien oui songe combattant
Two dark eyes look down,		Qu'un œil noir te regarde
And love is your reward.		Et que l'amour t'attend.

José has stabbed Carmen . . . She falls dead. José kneels beside her . . . The curtain to the arena opens. The crowd comes out of the bullring.

JOSE
(rising)

You can take me away . . . I am the one who killed her.	Vous pouvez m'arrêter . . . C'est moi qui l'ai tuée.

(Escamillo appears on the steps of the bullring . . .)

Ah! Carmen! My Carmen . . . I adore you! [3a]	Ah, Carmen! ma Carmen adorée!

Curtain.

---

* Bizet originally indicated that Don José stabbed Carmen at this point so that she collapsed on his arm at the moment that the chorus was heard from the bullring.

Pantomime from Act One, Scene One.

This *'pantomime'* for Morales is in the 1875 vocal score (which was corrected by Bizet) but not in the full scores. According to Fritz Oeser (p. 721 of his Introductory Notes in the Bärenreiter Vocal Score) it was inserted for the leading lyric baritone at the Opéra Comique, Duvernoy, whom they badly needed in the cast to give authority to the difficult small part of Corporal Morales. Duvernoy himself probably insisted on an aria. This Bizet put in for the first performance: as he probably did not envisage it being used with later casts, he did not include it in his M.S. full score. Because it obviously had no part in the dramatic structure of the opera in his mind, it has seemed proper to take it out of the text.

Morales was also included in the supper party at the Inn in Act Two to give him more to do, although as a Corporal, he would arguably not have been included in an officers' party. In the full score, but not in the vocal score, Andres who sang the tenor line in the ensemble to Escamillo's couplets, is still left in, as the part had not been changed to baritone for Morales.

During the preceding scene with Micaela the passers-by had stopped moving about the stage, but now they start crossing and re-crossing in a lively manner. Amongst the people who walk to and fro is an old gentleman who has offered his arm to a young lady . . . The old gentleman would like to continue his walk, but the young lady is doing all she can to keep him in the same place. She seems worried and anxious. She looks to the right, then to the left. She is waiting for someone and this someone has not appeared. This mime must match exactly the following verses.

MORALES

I

Just look at that! Shh! Just look at that! Stop the talk!	Attention! chut! Attention! Taisons-nous!
Old husband taking wife for a walk . . .	Voici venir un vieil époux,
Mistrustful eye . . . jealous expression . . .	Œil soupçonneux, mine jalouse,
Young wife held tight . . . She shan't escape him . . .	Il tient au bras sa jeune épouse;
Her lover, doubtless, hovers near . . .	L'amant sans doute n'est pas loin;
Waits round the corner to appear!	Il va sortir de quelque coin!

(Just at this moment a young man hurriedly enters the square.)

Ha! ha! ha! ha! There you are!	Ah! ah! ah! ah! Le voilà.

CHORUS

Let's wait and see the end of the affair!	Voyons, voyons comment ça tournera!

The second verse continues and matches exactly the scene being mimed by the three people. The young man approaches the old man and the young lady, bows, and whispers some words in a low voice, etc . . .

MORALES

II

(imitating the young man's assiduous attention)	
"Oh what a joy to find you here!"	Vous trouver ici, quel bonheur!
(imitating the old husband's grim appearance)	
"I am your humble servant, sir!"	Je suis bien votre serviteur.
(once more imitating the young man's manner)	
Our lover bows, with airs and graces.	Il salue, il parle avec grâce.
(now the old husband's manner)	
The old man stands there pulling faces.	Le vieux mari fait la grimace;
(imitating the young lady's leading demeanour)	
With charming smiles to lead him on	Mais d'un air fort encourageant
The lady welcomes her young man.	La dame acceuille le galant.

125

At this moment the young man takes a love letter out of his pocket and shows it to the lady. The husband, the young lady and the lover take a turn around the square slowly. The young man seeks an opportunity to give his love letter to the lady.

MORALES

III

They start to saunter round the square . . .	Ils font ensemble quelques pas;
Our lover points up in the air	Notre amoureux, levant le bras,
Above their heads as a diversion . . .	Faire voir au mari quelque chose,
Disgruntled husband's full attention	Et le mari, toujours morose,
Is on the sky . . . the trick was grand!	Regarde en l'air . . . le tour est fait!
He has slipped a note in her hand!	Car la dame a pris le billet!

The young man points out something in the air to the husband, whilst he passes the letter to the lady with the other hand.

ALL

(*laughing*)

We know the end of this affair!	On voit comment ça tournera.
Ha! ha! ha! ha!	Ah! ah! ah! ah!
Ha! ha! ha! ha!	Ah! ah! ah! ah!
We know the end of this affair!	On voit comment ça tournera.

Bugles and fifes can be heard faintly in the distance playing a military march. The old gentleman and the young man shake hands cordially and the young man salutes the lady respectfully. An officer comes out of the guardroom, etc. (continue with Act One, scene two)

Discography / *Martin Hoyle* All complete versions are in stereo and ir French. For comparative analysis and for a guide to the many excerpts on record, the enthusiast is referred to *Opera on Record* (ed. Alan Blyth Hutchinson, 1979)

Conductor Company/Orchestra	*Beecham* Paris ORTF	*Schippers* Suisse Romande	*Maazel* Deutsche Oper, Berlin	*Bernstein* Metropolitan Opera, New York	*Prêtre* Duclos Chorus, Paris Opéra
Carmen	De los Angeles	Resnik	Moffo	Horne	Callas
Don José	Gedda	Del Monaco	Corelli	McCracken	Gedda
Escamillo	Blanc	Krause	Cappucc.lli	Krause	Massard
Micaela	Micheau	Sutherland	Donath	Maliponte	Guiot
Disc UK number	SLS5021	SET256-8			SLS913
Tape UK number	TC-SLS5021				
Excerpts (disc)	ESD7047	SPA539			ASD2282
Excerpts (tape)	TC-ESD7047	KCSP539			
Disc US number	S3613	LON1368	300197	2709 043	S-3650X
Tape US number			500197	3371 006	4X3S-3650
Excerpts (disc) US	S35818			2530 534	S-36312
Excerpts (tape) US					4XS-36312

Conductor	Frübeck de Burgos	Karajan	Solti	Abbado	Lombard
Company/Orchestra	Paris Opéra	Vienna State Opera	Alldis Choir, LPO	Ambrosian Singers, LSO	Opéra du Rhin, Strasbourg Phil.
Carmen	Bumbry	L. Price	Troyanos	Berganza	Crespin
Don José	Vickers	Corelli	Domingo	Domingo	Py
Escamillo	Paskalis	Merrill	van Dam	Milnes	van Dam
Micaela	Freni	Freni	Te Kanawa	Cotrubas	Pilou
Disc UK number	ICI97 02072-4	SER5600	D11D3	2709 083	
Tape UK number		RK40004	K11K33	3371 040	
Excerpts (disc)			SET621	2537 049	
Excerpts (tape)			KCET621	3306 049	
Disc US number	S-3767	LSC-6199	13115	2709 083	70900/2
Tape US number		ARK3-2542	5-13115	3371 040	
Excerpts (disc) US		2843		0 2351170	
Excerpts (tape) US		RK-1036		3301 1710	